Linking Wilderness Research and Management

Volume 5—Understanding and Managing Backcountry Recreation Impacts on Terrestrial Wildlife:

An Annotated Reading List

Series Editor:

Vita Wright, Research Application Program Leader,
Aldo Leopold Wilderness Research Institute, Missoula, MT
Rocky Mountain Research Station
U.S. Department of Agriculture, Forest Service

Authors:

Douglas Tempel, Ecology Specialist[a]
Vita Wright, Program Leader
Janet Neilson, Ecology Specialist[b]
Tammy Mildenstein, Ecology Specialist

Research Application Program
Aldo Leopold Wilderness Research Institute, Missoula, MT
Rocky Mountain Research Station
U.S. Department of Agriculture, Forest Service

[a] Currently, Research Fellow, Department of Fisheries, Wildlife, & Conservation
Biology, University of Minnesota, St. Paul, MN.
[b] Currently, Wildlife Biologist, Glacier Bay National Park and Preserve, Gustavus,
AK.

USDA Forest Service
General Technical Report RMRS-GTR-79-vol. 5.

September 2008

Authors

Douglas Tempel is a Research Fellow and Ph.D. candidate at the University of Minnesota in St. Paul. In this position, he serves as the Project Leader on a California spotted owl demography study in the central Sierra Nevada. He also researched spotted owl fecal hormone levels for his M.S. in Wildlife Conservation from the University of Minnesota, which he received in 2002. He became interested in managing recreation impacts on wildlife during his time as a Wilderness Ranger in Utah's High Uintas Wilderness from 1995-1997.

Vita Wright is Research Application Program Leader at the U.S. Forest Service, Rocky Mountain Research Station, Aldo Leopold Wilderness Research Institute. She obtained her M.S. in Organismal Biology and Ecology in 1996 after conducting a multi-scale analysis of Flammulated Owl habitat use. She has worked as a Research Application Specialist since 1998. Currently working on her Ph.D. through the University of Montana, College of Forestry and Conservation, she is studying individual and organizational influences to the use of science by federal agency managers.

Janet Neilson has worked as a Wildlife Biologist for Glacier Bay National Park's humpback whale monitoring program since 1997. This program provides information on whale behavior and distribution needed for the management of recreational and commercial vessels in the park. Janet obtained her M.S. in marine biology in 2005 with a thesis on humpback whale entanglement in fishing gear. She has conducted field research on a number of terrestrial birds, including raptors and woodpeckers.

Tammy Mildenstein is an Ecology Specialist at the U.S. Forest Service, Rocky Mountain Research Station, Aldo Leopold Wilderness Research Institute and a Ph.D. candidate at the University of Montana. She received an M.S. in wildlife biology at the University of Montana in 2002 for her research on habitat use of endangered flying foxes in the Philippines. Her dissertation research follows on her conservation efforts of Philippine flying foxes; she is now studying the population level impacts of human disturbance on several flying fox species. Tammy's interest in managing recreation impacts on wildlife comes both from her experiences in the Philippines, where anthropogenic disturbance plays a large role in the decline of flying foxes, and from her backyard in Missoula, which is a heavily-used national recreation area.

Preface

Federal land management agencies have recognized the importance of incorporating the best available scientific knowledge into management decisions. However, both managers and researchers have struggled to identify effective processes for achieving this objective. The Aldo Leopold Wilderness Research Institute's Research Application Program works toward understanding barriers to the use of science in management and develops ways to make relevant scientific information more accessible. Managers can base their decisions on the best available scientific knowledge only if they are aware of current and relevant science and how it relates to their management goals.

The *Linking Wilderness Research and Management* series of annotated reading lists was developed to help land managers and others access scientific information relevant to protecting and restoring wilderness and similarly managed lands and the myriad values associated with such lands. References in these reading lists have been categorized to draw attention to the relevance of each publication and then organized to provide a logical framework for addressing the issue. Each volume begins with the references necessary to understand the overall issue and then provides references useful for identifying management goals, understanding influences on those goals, and selecting and implementing management approaches. This volume begins with a section highlighting the importance of wilderness for wildlife conservation and the value of wildlife for backcountry recreationists. The second section provides a conceptual overview for understanding potential recreation impacts on wildlife. The third section contains specific studies on recreation impacts on wildlife with a focus on recreational uses that occur in backcountry areas. The fourth section reviews planning frameworks and techniques relevant to managing backcountry recreation impacts on wildlife. A final section contains additional resources such as web sites and annotated bibliographies.

These reading lists were designed to serve a wide audience. First, each list introduces generalists to the breadth of factors that should be considered when addressing management issues. These volumes also enable specialists to maintain familiarity with research relevant to their discipline but outside their area of expertise. For instance, this volume may be useful to a biologist who manages a particular species but is not familiar with the human disturbance literature. For those readers already well-versed on an issue, this series facilitates access to literature that can add depth to their conceptual knowledge. Rather than produce comprehensive bibliographies, which may be unwieldy for those with limited time, the authors have limited their annotations to review articles, the most recent literature, and frequently cited classic publications. These lists can serve as a starting point for readers seeking more detail on a topic when conducting their own literature reviews.

To facilitate access to these lists and enable us to update them, the lists are also available through the Aldo Leopold Wilderness Research Institute's Web site: http://leopold.wilderness.net/resapp.htm. The Leopold Institute is a Federal interagency research institute that focuses on ecological and social science research needed to sustain wilderness ecosystems and wilderness values. I hope this series will help sustain wilderness and similarly managed lands and their associated values by enabling managers, policymakers, educators, user groups, and others to access the best available science on the topics covered.

—Vita Wright, Series Editor

Acknowledgments

We thank Doug Whittaker, Brett Walker, Jeff Marion, Yu-Fai Leung, Peter Landres, Steve Gniadek, Brian Glaspell, David Cole, and Chris Barns for reviews and helpful comments on earlier versions of this manuscript. Supplementary funding was received from the U.S. Fish and Wildlife Service, Bureau of Land Management, and interagency Arthur Carhart National Wilderness Training Center.

Contents

INTRODUCTION

The large increase in outdoor recreation activity over the last 50 years has been recognized as a potentially serious threat to North American wildlife populations. Threats to wildlife in wilderness are a concern to backcountry recreationists as well as the American public. The protection of wildlife habitat and endangered species was one of the most highly valued benefits of wilderness according to a telephone survey of approximately 1,900 people in the United States (Cordell and others 1998). Many backcountry recreation users cite the opportunity to view wildlife as an important part of their wilderness experience. Threats to wildlife in wilderness are also a concern for wildlife preservation. Wilderness often provides a refuge for wildlife amid a matrix of more intensively developed lands, and is especially valuable for wide-ranging species that are sensitive to human disturbance and those that depend on special habitats found predominantly in wilderness (Hendee and Mattson 2002).

Impacts of recreation on wildlife include increased energetic demands during critical periods of the year, loss of habitat through avoidance of areas of human activity, exposure to predators while avoiding humans, and loss of habitat through changes in vegetation resulting from recreation activities (Knight and Gutzwiller 1995). If widespread, cumulative impacts on individuals of a species may ultimately affect local and regional populations. Changes in species' populations may affect wildlife communities, especially if the impacted species have strong interactions with other species.

The management of wilderness recreation impacts on wildlife in designated wilderness is complicated by the potentially conflicting mandates of The Wilderness Act of 1964 [Public Law 88-577]. The Act mandates the preservation of natural conditions in wilderness while requiring managers to provide opportunities for primitive recreation. However, when recreation affects wildlife species, populations, or communities, it can hinder the preservation of natural conditions. To address the dual mandates, appropriate wilderness recreational activities must not only be provided, but must be managed to minimize their impacts on wildlife, and more broadly, to wilderness ecosystems. Wilderness managers can use direct approaches such as restricting visitor numbers, activities, or access in some areas. In backcountry areas outside of designated wilderness, manipulating wildlife and wildlife habitat may be appropriate. Indirect approaches may also be used, such as visitor education and the careful location and design of trails, trailheads, and adjacent roads and campgrounds.

We have compiled this annotated list of references to help wildlife, wilderness, and recreation managers better understand backcountry recreation impacts on wildlife and be informed of the variety of management tools available for minimizing impacts. Managing recreation impacts on wildlife is an interdisciplinary issue, with management decisions affecting both wildlife and visitors. We have designed this reading list to cross disciplinary boundaries. The reading list includes literature from the wildlife discipline, such as papers needed to understand impacts on wildlife, as well as literature from the recreation discipline that is needed to understand recreation management techniques.

Whereas many of the papers included in this reading list present original research or summarize the results of multiple studies, other papers are conceptual. Conclusions and recommendations in the annotations have been extracted from the original works. Rather than promote some concepts over others, we have attempted to reflect the range of published literature on this topic.

While researching this topic, we noted several information gaps in the existing literature. The vast majority of research has reported short-term responses of individual animals to recreational activities and used this information to project potential impacts on wildlife populations or communities. Although measured responses have sometimes included demographic variables such as reproductive output or fledging success, we are aware of very few studies that have collected extensive data over several years to provide a true estimate of potential impacts on population rates of change. In addition, previous research has focused almost solely on mammals and birds, especially charismatic species (bears, raptors, colony-nesting birds) and game species (deer, elk, waterfowl). We suggest the expansion of future research to include other animal species that may be important to local ecosystems and/or have restricted ranges that overlap extensively with areas of high recreational use. Finally, previous studies on wildlife responses to primitive recreational activities have focused mainly on hiking. Managers would benefit from additional research on activities such as horseback riding, rock climbing, cross-country skiing, and kayaking in marine coastal areas.

SCOPE

This reading list focuses on primitive recreational activities (for example, hiking, camping, wildlife viewing, and rock climbing) that have the potential to impact terrestrial wildlife in wilderness and similarly managed areas. Although hunting can also impact wildlife populations in wilderness, we have only included references on indirect hunting impacts, such as displacement of wildlife from suitable habitat. We have not included research on the population effects of hunting-induced mortality. This topic is large enough that it would warrant its own reading list. Motorized recreation is prohibited in designated wilderness. With the following exceptions, we have not included references related to motorized transport. References on aircraft overflights have been included because these are common in some wilderness areas and National Parks. Several snowmobile papers are included either because they demonstrate the use of an innovative technique for assessing wildlife responses to disturbance (for example, using stress hormones) or because they also refer to the effects of nonmotorized recreation use. Additionally, several papers addressing the effects of roads have been included where they either refer to roads adjacent to reserves or to roads that cut through backcountry areas of National Parks or similar reserves. We hope these resources, as well as databases available at the following websites, http://www.montanatws.org/chapters/mt/pages/page4b html and http://www.wildlandscpr.org, will help readers managing backcountry areas with motorized use to access additional literature on the topic.

Although there is some overlap, this volume is different from Volume 2 in this series, *Defining, managing, and monitoring wilderness visitor experiences: an annotated reading list* (Glaspell and Puttkammer 2001). Whereas Volume 2 focused on understanding and managing visitor experiences (for example, visitors desires, influences to their actual experiences, and techniques for managing and monitoring those experiences), the recreation part of Volume 5 broadly covers the strategies and techniques used to manage recreation impacts. While many of the readings in the management section do not directly address wildlife, we have included them to increase understanding of visitor management techniques that may be used to protect wildlife. Readings included in this section are intended to provide a basic understanding of recreation management techniques, the reasoning behind them, and their assumptions. Volume 2 is focused more narrowly on managing visitor experiences. Our intent with Volume 5 is to facilitate access to references that will (1) increase understanding of backcountry recreation impacts on wildlife and (2) familiarize readers with various recreation management approaches.

This reading list is not a comprehensive bibliography, but instead offers a broad overview of the topic using the best examples we found in the literature. Where possible, we have favored more recent references. Readers can identify older papers of interest from the citations contained in newer papers. We do include references to older articles when they illustrate a concept particularly well or serve as a classic reference for a given species or group. Had we added depth, we would have defeated our purpose of providing readers with a manageable list of references. For a more comprehensive list, we refer readers to an online bibliography produced by the Montana Chapter of The Wildlife Society (http://www.montanatws.org/chapters/mt/pages/page4b html).

We have focused on research conducted in North America, although international research has been included when it illustrates a concept well or little North American research exists on a particular topic. In addition, the sections for poorly studied species or taxonomic groups (for example, reptiles and amphibians) contain a greater proportion of the existing literature than sections for well-studied species (for example, bald eagles).

Most of the literature in this bibliography was obtained prior to Summer 2006. Although there will always be new literature relevant to individual taxa, the framework provided for approaching this management issue (as evident in the table of contents) is based on decades of research by both wildlife and recreation scientists. As such, it will continue to be a valid framework for describing and managing recreation impacts on wildlife. For readers interested in using either scientific abstract databases or Internet search engines to locate more recent literature, we recommend using the following general terms for locating publications on impacts: wildlife (or the taxon of interest) and disturbance and recreation. The following general terms will provide a useful starting point for publications on recreation and/or for narrowing the search to focus on backcountry: recreation trends, recreation management techniques, backcountry, wilderness, protected areas, or national parks. When using the Internet, it will be most efficient to use search engines designed to conduct research, academic, or scholar searches for scientific publications (for examples see UCLA Library 2008, Zillman 2004). Some of these will have the option of identifying the timeframe of interest (for example, 2006 – present).

ORGANIZATION

This reading list is organized into a framework for understanding backcountry recreation impacts on wildlife. Specifically,

Section I illustrates (1) the value of wilderness for wildlife conservation and (2) the value of wildlife for backcountry recreationists.

Section II provides an overview of potential impacts at a number of levels: individual, population, and community. Indirect effects of recreation on wildlife habitat and methods for assessing recreation impacts are also addressed in this section.

Section III offers specific examples of research on backcountry recreation impacts on a wide range of mammal, bird, reptile, amphibian, and invertebrate species.

Section IV provides an overview of strategies, management planning frameworks, and techniques for minimizing backcountry recreation impacts on wildlife, as well as references illustrating their application.

Section V gives additional resources, such as online databases and other Web sites, and annotated bibliographies.

Indices are also provided for readers wishing to locate articles by a particular author or for a specific type of recreational activity. For each of the major subsections within Sections I through V, we provide a short summary of the subsection's contents followed by an annotated list of references alphabetized by author. Some references are relevant to multiple topics and are listed in two or more sections. The full annotation is given once in the most pertinent section. In other sections, we provide a cross-reference to the page where the full annotation can be found.

Author names do not necessarily appear in the same format throughout the list because the names are formatted in accordance with the original works. In addition, we include scientific names only when they appear in the original reference. We use the common and scientific names as they appeared in the original article rather than changing species names to reflect current classification schemes.

OBTAINING CITED PUBLICATIONS

We recognize that it may be difficult for those in the field to obtain many of the readings included in this reading list. For those with access to local public or University libraries, books and journal articles can be obtained through interlibrary loan programs. For those who work in remote locations, there are several government resources that provide document delivery (free to Federal employees in the United States). A current list of these resources can be found on the Aldo Leopold Wilderness Research Institute's website (http://leopold.wilderness net/library.htm). They include:

- Bureau of Land Management Library (http://www.blm. gov/nstc/library/library html)
- National Agricultural Library (http://www nal.usda.gov/ services/request.shtml)
- National Forest Service Library (http://fsweb.wo.fs fed. us/library)
- National Park Service Library (http://library.nps.gov)
- USDA Digital Desktop Library (http://www nal.usda. gov/digitop)
- USDA FS Research Publications (http://www.treesearch. fs fed.us)
- USDOI Library (http://library.doi.gov/ill.html)
- U.S. Fish and Wildlife Service Conservation Library (http://library.fws.gov)

In addition, electronic versions of articles can often be located immediately by typing the author and year, or several words of the title, into an Internet Search Engine.

REFERENCES

Cordell, H. Ken; Tarrant, Michael A.; McDonald, Barbara L.; Bergstrom, John C. 1998. How the public views wilderness: more results from the USA survey on recreation and the environment. International Journal of Wilderness. 4(3):28-31.

Glaspell, Brian; Puttkammer, Annette 2001. Linking Wilderness Research and Management—volume 2. Defining, managing, and monitoring wilderness visitor experiences: an annotated reading list. Fort Collins, CO: U.S. Department of Agriculture, Forest Service, Rocky Mountain Research Station. Gen. Tech. Rep. RMRS-GTR-79-Vol 2. 29 p.

Hendee, John C.; Mattson, David J. 2002. Wildlife in wilderness: a North American and international perspective. In: Hendee, John C.; Dawson, Chad P., eds. Wilderness management: stewardship and protection of resources and values. 3d ed. Golden, CO: Fulcrum Publishing:321-349.

Knight, Richard L.; Gutzwiller, Kevin J., eds. 1995. Wildlife and recreationists: coexistence through management and research. Washington, DC: Island Press. 372 p.

UCLA Library. 2008. Google Scholar™, search engines, databases, and the research process. [Online]. Available: http://www2.library.ucla.edu/googlescholar/index.cfm. [2008, April 28].

Zillman, Marcus P. 2004. Academic and scholar search engines and sources. Unpublished white paper. [Online]. Available: http://zillman.blogspot.com/2004/12/academic-and-scholar-search-engines html [2008, April 25].

ANNOTATED READING LIST

I. Why Manage Backcountry Recreation Impacts on Wildlife?

A. VALUE OF BACKCOUNTRY FOR WILDLIFE CONSERVATION

Wilderness areas are important to the future persistence of the species and/or populations that use wilderness, because they 1) provide good quality habitat that is relatively free from human disturbance, 2) are relatively large, harboring many species and habitat types, and 3) are protected in the long term (Hendee and Mattson 2002; Mackey and others 1998; Noss 1990; Sala and others 2000). Especially benefited are wilderness dependent species (Hendee and Mattson 2002, Mattson 1997) such as large ranging carnivores (Noss 1990), local endemics (Mittermeier and others 2003), threatened species, and species of limited distribution that rely on the wilderness area as their habitat (Mackey and others 1998).

Additionally, the protective measures of wilderness areas go beyond the numbers of species, populations, and individuals for which they provide habitat, to the protection of entire ecosystems (Mackey and others 1998, Noss 1990). The large-scale, long-term protection of wilderness areas not only allows for the ecological connections of functioning ecosystems, but also provides a venue for the continuation of evolutionary processes (Hendee and Mattson 2002, Noss 1990). The ecological integrity of an intact ecosystem ensures its sustainability and strengthens its resilience to environmental change (Mackey and others 1998), especially to human disturbance such as climate change (Jensen 2000, Walther and others 2002).

Finally, wilderness areas are an important resource for wildlife managers. Not only do they offer core reserves for species of concern (Noss 1990), but they also serve as a natural reference for managers of wildlife populations in more perturbed environments (Leopold 1941, Noss 1990).

Hendee, John C.; Mattson, David J. 2002. Wildlife in wilderness: a North American and international perspective. In: Hendee, John C.; Dawson, Chad P., eds. Wilderness management: stewardship and protection of resources and values. 3d ed. Golden, CO: Fulcrum Publishing:321–349.

Annotation: In this chapter, the authors emphasize that certain indigenous wildlife species require, or heavily depend upon, wilderness. Four categories of wilderness wildlife are given: (1) wilderness-dependent wildlife, (2) wilderness-associated wildlife, (3) common native wildlife found in wilderness, and (4) exotic or nonnative species found in wilderness. To maintain their regional populations, wilderness-dependent species (for example, grizzly bears, wolverines, and Canada lynx) require either the refuge from human presence or the absence of roads, railways, and fences provided by wilderness. Wilderness-associated species either require habitat typically found in wilderness (for example, marmots) or are displaced to wilderness by human activities (for example, prairie dogs and black-footed ferrets). While these species' survival is not dependent upon wilderness, wilderness is a major factor in their conservation. The recreational, aesthetic, and economic importance of certain wildlife species found in wilderness are also discussed and some examples of studies related to these values are provided.

Jensen, Mari N. 2000. Climate warming shakes up species. BioScience. 54(8):722-729.

Annotation: In addition to impacts from human recreation, wildlife in wilderness areas is also subjected to large-scale human disturbance pervasive across protected area boundaries. This paper is a non-technical summary of documented evidence of wildlife responses to global climate change that might affect the use of reserves by wildlife. Long-term weather history data are available for areas around the globe, but long-term biological data sets are much more rare. Where there are long-term biological data, however, an effect from global warming is often evident. The author gives examples of changes in species characteristics (from over 229 plant species from the Boston arboretum and 400 species in England) and species geographic ranges (for example, pikas and bighorn sheep moving up in elevation and butterflies moving North in latitude) to cope with warming trends. She also discusses the results of modeling attempts to predict changes expected with climate change, including loss of endemic species, a restriction in range of remaining species, and at least an 18 percent reduction in biodiversity. Experts recommend that reserve designers and biodiversity managers prepare for anticipated habitat changes and plan for migration requirements in species.

Leopold, R. Aldo. 1941. Wilderness as a land laboratory. Living Wilderness. 6(July):3.

Annotation: In this brief but classic essay, Aldo Leopold argues the importance of wildernesses as land laboratories, or natural, unperturbed references to which managed lands can be compared. Leopold likens the complexity of natural ecosystems to the human body, in which symptoms may appear in one area but are caused by another part entirely. As with the medical field, Leopold says that conservation management often focuses on treating symptoms rather than looking at the true source of ecological failures. Protecting healthy, naturally functioning ecosystems, such as wildernesses, gives managers access to natural control areas from which they can make observations and learn about the ecological systems they aim to conserve.

Mackey, Brendan G.; Lesslie, Rob G.; Lindemayer, David B.; Nix, Henry A.; Incoll, Ryan D. 1998. The role of wilderness in nature conservation. A report to The Australian and World Heritage Group. Environment Australia. [Online]. Available: http://www.heritage.gov.au/anlr/code/pubs/rolewild html [April 18, 2008].

Annotation: This report, prepared by biologists for The Australian and World Heritage Group, is a thorough discussion of the benefits of wilderness to wildlife and biodiversity conservation. The authors start with definitions of wilderness and biodiversity conservation and then outline the history of environmental conservation. They describe six major human-caused threats to biodiversity and natural ecosystems: changing fire and hydrological regimes, changing vegetative cover (land use), roads, introduced species, and accelerated global climate change. Wilderness areas, as the most strictly protected, play the important role of buffering natural ecosystems from these threats. The authors argue that wildlife managers should give ample attention to wilderness quality, which they define as the absence of negative human-caused impacts. The authors found that higher wilderness quality was correlated with smaller numbers of threatened species in protected areas. If reserves are going to play a role in wildlife conservation, they should be large enough to buffer against large-scale perturbations, spatially oriented to promote genetic flow and migration, representative of natural communities, and possess the highest possible ecological integrity.

Mattson, David J. 1997. Wilderness-dependent wildlife: the large and the carnivorous. International Journal of Wilderness. 3(4):34-38.

Annotation: Written for a non-technical audience, this is a brief discussion of the multiple benefits of wilderness to wildlife, especially to wilderness-dependent wildlife. Some wildlife species are particularly dependent on wilderness because of their vulnerability to human-caused mortality. Wilderness-dependent species tend to be large-bodied species because they: 1) typically occur at low densities and/or are at carrying capacity, 2) are more likely to pose threats to humans and human economic interests (for example, species that directly threaten humans, eat agricultural crops, or carry diseases that can affect livestock), and 3) are preferred by humans for meat. While humans kill wildlife for a number of reasons, globally, poverty and lack of education are emergent characteristics in human societies where wildlife species extinction risks are high. Conservation activities, therefore, must go beyond wilderness designation and management to interfacing more effectively with local human communities.

Mittermeier, Russell A.; Mittermeier, Cristina G.; Brooks, Thomas M.; Pilgrim, John D.; Konstant, William R.; da Fonseca, Gustavo A.B.; Kormos, Cyril. 2003. Wilderness and biodiversity conservation. Proceedings of the National Academy of Science. 100(18):10309-10313.

Annotation: This study assesses the biodiversity value of the world's remaining wilderness areas. The authors identified 24 intact ecosystems larger than 10,000 km^2, which have minimal human density, have greater than 70 percent of original forest cover remaining, and are representative of the world's eco-regions. The conservation of these areas will be especially important to the endemic plants (18 percent of the world's total plant species) and animals (10 percent of the world's total vertebrate species) that live in these areas. The biggest and most pervasive threats to the continued persistence of the ecosystems in these areas are agriculture, grazing, hunting, invasive species, logging, and mining.

Noss, Reed F. 1990. What can wilderness do for biodiversity? In: Reed, Patrick C., comp. Preparing to manage wilderness in the 21st century: proceedings of the conference; 1990 April 4–6; Athens, GA. Gen. Tech. Rep. SE-66. Asheville, NC: U.S. Department of Agriculture, Forest Service, Southeastern Forest Experiment Station: 49–61. [Online]. Available: http://www.srs.fs.usda.gov/pubs/gtr/gtr_se066.pdf [April 18, 2008].

Annotation: This paper, which was presented at the Forest Service conference *Preparing to Manage Wilderness in the 21st Century* outlines how wilderness benefits biodiversity conservation on several levels. Genetic diversity is promoted through large and interconnected protected areas. Species diversity is higher in wilderness areas, because both vulnerable native species and those less vulnerable are maintained in these protected areas. Ecological communities are especially conserved in large wilderness areas, which provide venues for entire biological communities to interact under natural disturbance regimes. Finally, landscape-level diversity is dependent on the size of the protected area. Large wilderness areas may represent our only chance for maintaining the ecological gradients that harbor native biodiversity on a landscape scale.

Sala, Osvaldo E.; Chapin, F. Steward, III; Armesto, Juan J.; Berlow, Eric; Bloomfield, Janine; Dirzo, Rodolfo; Huber-Sanwald, Elisabeth; Huenneke, Laura F.; Jackson, Robert B.; Kinzig, Ann; Leemans, Rick; Lodge, David M.; Mooney, Harold A.; Oesterheld, Martin; Poff, N. Leroy; Sykes, Martin T.; Walker, Brian H.; Walker, Marilyn; Wall, Diana H. 2000. Global biodiversity scenarios for the year 2100. Science. 287:1770-1774.

Annotation: Many types of human disturbance have large enough impacts to pervade across protected area boundaries. This paper describes predicted future changes to biodiversity given current trends in disturbance caused by humans. Using models, the authors investigated large-scale disturbance regimes such as climate change and acid rain, more localized disturbances such as land use changes and the introduction of invasive species, as well as interactions between multiple disturbance causes. In terrestrial ecosystems, they found that land use change (for example, conversion of tropical forests to grasslands) was the largest driver of loss of biodiversity followed by climate change. The authors also found an interactive effect among drivers of biodiversity change. In order to mitigate negative changes to biodiversity, they recommend that managers strive to reduce the driving forces at the global scale as well as tailor management on the local scale according to the biological, social, and economic characteristics of the region involved.

Walther, Gian-Reto; Post, Eric; Convey, Peter; Menzel, Annette; Parmesan, Camille; Beebee, Trevor J.C.; Fromentin, Jean-Marc; Hoegh-Guldberg, Ove; Bairlein, Franz. 2002. Ecological responses to recent climate change. Nature 416:389-395.

Annotation: Managers of recreational impacts on backcountry wildlife need to be aware of other human-caused stresses on these systems, such as the ecological impacts of global warming. Despite uncertainty in how global climates are expected to change, the authors list evidence of past climate change impacts on wildlife across a wide range of species and geographical distributions. They group wildlife responses to climate change into four types: 1) phenology and physiology of organisms have been altered, particularly prominent in the literature is the earlier onset of springtime breeding behaviors, 2) the range and distribution of species have pushed toward the North and South Poles and higher elevations, 3) the composition of species and interactions within communities have changed with some species tracking climate change out of old and into new ecological communities, and 4) the structure and dynamics of ecosystems have been altered by variations in life history traits and the resulting changes in species' populations dynamics. These changes suggest wilderness and protected areas will play key roles in the future, as ecosystems in these areas may be left to adjust to environmental changes.

B. VALUE OF WILDLIFE TO BACKCOUNTRY RECREATIONISTS

Wildlife viewing is a major component of a quality wilderness experience for wilderness users across the country (Brooks and others 1999; Brown and others 1980; Decker and others 1991; Roggenbuck and others 1993; Shafer and Hammitt 1994; Virden and Schreyer 1988). Many species that are associated with wilderness areas (for example, bears, elk, bighorn sheep) inspire and fascinate people.

For example, visitors are willing to spend large amounts of money to view Alaskan brown bears (*Ursus arctos*) in a wilderness setting where visitor numbers are restricted (Clayton and Mendelsohn 1993). Other wilderness visitors have expressed strong support for management actions restricting recreation activities for the benefit of bighorn sheep (*Ovis canadensis mexicana*; Harris and others 1995a). Among the general public, backcountry recreationists are also more interested in viewing wildlife than other segments of the public (Manfredo and Larson 1993, Martin 1995). Nonetheless, the American public considers the protection of wildlife habitat to be one of the major functions of Federally designated wilderness areas (Cordell and others 1998). The public also places a high value on "nonconsumptive" uses of wildlife (see Wilkes 1997 in Section II.A. for a critique of this term) that do not directly remove individuals from the population (Arthur and Wilson 1979).

Arthur, Louise M.; Wilson, W. Robert. 1979. Assessing the demand for wildlife resources: a first step. Wildlife Society Bulletin. 7(1): 30-34.

Annotation: The authors summarize three surveys that compare public attitudes toward consumptive and nonconsumptive uses of wildlife. In a telephone survey of the general public, nonconsumptive uses of wildlife (wildlife viewing, appreciation for the existence of wildlife, and the maintenance of ecosystems) were rated as much more important than consumptive uses (hunting, food, and fur) by respondents, including those who approved of hunting. In two mail surveys of hunters and fishermen, respondents indicated that enjoyment of the outdoor environment was the main reason for participating in such activities. According to the authors, these results highlight the need for managers to protect wildlife habitat and provide the public with wildlife viewing opportunities.

Brooks, Jeffrey J.; Warren, Robert J.; Nelms, M. G.; Tarrant, Michael A. 1999. Visitor attitudes toward and knowledge of restored bobcats on Cumberland Island National Seashore, Georgia. Wildlife Society Bulletin. 27(4):1089-1097.

Annotation: The authors surveyed four user groups (backcountry campers, developed-site campers, day visitors, and deer hunters) to determine their attitudes toward a restored bobcat (*Lynx rufus*) population. Bobcats were successfully reintroduced to Cumberland Island 8 years prior to the survey. Eighty-seven percent of all respondents indicated that seeing wildlife was moderately, very, or extremely important to their decision to visit Cumberland Island. The authors report that backcountry campers had the most positive attitude score toward bobcats, although their score was not statistically different from the developed-site campers or day visitors. On a bobcat knowledge quiz, respondents had a mean score of 3.8 out of 10. The low score was attributed to the visitors' lack of direct experience with bobcats. The authors recommend that managers provide visitors with information displays focused on carnivores and other elusive species of social or ecological concern.

Brown, Perry J.; Haas, Glenn E.; Driver, B. L. 1980. Value of wildlife to wilderness users. In: Proceedings of the second conference on scientific research in the National Parks; 1979 November 26–30, San Francisco, CA. Washington, DC: National Park Service; Springfield, VA: National Technical Information Service. 6:168-179.

Annotation: The authors surveyed visitors to three Colorado wilderness areas to determine the desired psychological outcomes of their visits and the importance of different physical resources to achieving these outcomes. The most important psychological outcome was to establish a relationship with nature. Visitors were then grouped according to the importance they placed on different desired outcomes. Wildlife was one of several physical resources that contributed strongly to the recreational experience for all visitor groups; the others were lakes and streams, vegetation, and attractive topography. Different visitor groups varied in their appreciation for particular types of wildlife (for example, deer, birds, fish), but they consistently appreciated large wildlife species the most.

Clayton, Creed; Mendelsohn, Robert. 1993. The value of watchable wildlife: a case study of McNeil River. Journal of Environmental Management. 39:101-106.

Annotation: The authors surveyed visitors at McNeil River Falls in Alaska to assess the economic value of bear viewing at this site. Each summer at this game sanctuary, a regulated number of visitors view the unusually high concentration of Alaskan brown bears (*Ursus arctos*). At the time of this study, visitors paid up to $50 for a permit to view the bears, and some visitors paid over $1000 in transportation costs. Visitors were asked two open-ended and two discrete-choice questions, each designed to estimate how much money they would be willing to pay for a bear-viewing permit. After adjusting for outliers and combining the results from all questions, the authors indicated that people would be willing to pay an average of $250 for a guaranteed permit.

Cordell, H. Ken; Tarrant, Michael A.; McDonald, Barbara L.; Bergstrom, John C. 1998. How the public views wilderness: more results from the USA survey on recreation and the environment. International Journal of Wilderness. 4(3):28-31.

Annotation: In a telephone survey of more than 1,900 people in the United States over age 15, respondents were asked about the importance of 13 benefits or values derived from wilderness protection. Two of the most highly valued wilderness benefits were the protection of wildlife habitat and the protection of endangered species. Seventy-nine percent and 74 percent of respondents, respectively, rated these benefits as "very" or "extremely important." In contrast, 49 percent considered recreation opportunities to be to be a "very" or "extremely important" benefit. In general, benefits associated with wilderness protection were considered to be more important than benefits related to wilderness use.

Decker, Daniel J.; Connelly, Nancy A.; Brown, Tommy L.; Smolka, Robert A., Jr. 1991. The importance of wildlife in wildland visitation and recreation satisfaction. Transactions of the Northeastern Section of The Wildlife Society. 48:39-48.

Annotation: The authors surveyed over 1,000 visitors to northern New York to determine the importance of wildlife for planning and enjoying their visit to the area. All types of visitors were surveyed, including backcountry recreationists. The region is dominated by the 2.4-million Ha Adirondack Park, which is largely managed as a roadless preserve. Nature viewing was cited as the most important reason for visiting the area, and viewing wildlife was a moderately important component of nature viewing. In addition, 45 percent of the respondents observed or photographed wildlife during their visit. Overall, trip satisfaction was positively correlated with the quality of a visitor's wildlife viewing experience. The authors recommend that managers provide more educational material to increase visitor appreciation for wildlife.

Grinnell, Joseph; Storer, Tracy I. 1916. Animal life as an asset of national parks. Science. 44:375-380.

Annotation: In this early paper, the authors emphasize the importance of National Parks to recreation and scientific research. At the time, outdoor recreation was becoming increasingly important to society because of the rapid industrialization and urbanization occurring in the United States. Wildlife was thought to be among the most important recreational assets of National Parks, providing visitors with auditory and visual stimuli, a sense of connection with the natural world, and a curiosity to learn more about the natural world. At a time when some large predators were still being eliminated from National Parks, the authors called for the protection of all native wildlife in Parks.

Harris, Lisa K.; Krausman, Paul R.; Shaw, William W. 1995a. Human attitudes and mountain sheep in a wilderness setting. Wildlife Society Bulletin. 23(1):66-72.

Annotation: In the Pusch Ridge Wilderness adjacent to Tuscon, Arizona, the authors surveyed hikers along two heavily used trails to assess their attitudes toward conserving mountain sheep (*Ovis canadensis mexicana*). This Wilderness supported a regionally important sheep population that declined markedly during the preceding 50 years. Most respondents (83 percent) had previously visited the Wilderness, and 79 percent reported watching wildlife during their visit. In addition, most respondents (93 percent) were aware of the mountain sheep in the Wilderness, although only 15 percent had actually seen them. Respondents expressed strong support for future management actions (dog control, prescribed burning, and recreational closures) to protect the sheep, even though these actions would restrict or affect recreational use of the Wilderness.

Hendee, John C.; Mattson, David J. 2002. Wildlife in wilderness: a North American and international perspective. In: Hendee, John C.; Dawson, Chad P., eds. Wilderness management: stewardship and protection of resources and values. 3d ed. Golden, CO: Fulcrum Publishing:321-349.

Annotation: The authors recognize that wildlife is an integral component of wilderness character, as a reflection of ecological and cultural conditions. Culturally, they describe how wilderness quality can be diminished with the loss of key wildlife species (for example, grizzlies, wolves, caribou). Ecologically, they note that wilderness quality is reflected in the presence of wilderness-dependent wildlife species that require areas with minimal human activity, such as megaherbivores, large carnivores, and migratory ungulates. Additionally, the authors reference the following examples of wildlife species that play a role in maintaining wilderness ecosystems: alligators, elephants, grizzly bears, wild pigs. They conclude that wilderness wildlife has recreation, educational, aesthetic, economic, and political values.

Manfredo, Michael J.; Larson, Richard A. 1993. Managing for wildlife viewing recreation experiences: an application in Colorado. Wildlife Society Bulletin. 21(3):226-236.

Annotation: The authors used a preliminary phone survey of Denver area residents to identify persons interested in viewing wildlife who were willing to complete a more detailed mail survey. Mail survey respondents were classed into four groups (Types I, II, III, and IV) based on a cluster analysis of their primary reasons for viewing wildlife. Eighty-one percent of Type I respondents participated in wildlife viewing on a "regular basis," more than any other group. This group was also more likely to combine wildlife viewing with primitive recreational activities, such as camping, fishing, backpacking, mountain climbing, and cross-country skiing. Finally, Type I respondents expressed a much greater interest in receiving wildlife viewing information and being actively involved in the recreation planning process.

Martin, Steven R. 1995. Preferences for recreational wildlife viewing experiences: a survey of nonresident visitors to Montana. Res. Rep. 38. Missoula, MT: University of Montana, Institute for Tourism and Recreation Research. 45 p. *(Note: This document can be ordered by email at itrr@ forestry.umt.edu or by calling 406-243-5686.)*

Annotation: The author surveyed nonresident visitors to Montana to understand their preferences for wildlife viewing experiences. Based on their level of participation in wildlife viewing or personal commitment to wildlife conservation, respondents were categorized as high involvement (or wildlife viewing specialists), medium involvement, or low involvement. High-involvement visitors were more likely to be visiting Montana to see wildlife, more interested in viewing all wildlife species (not just "high-profile" species), and more interested in information about natural history and wildlife viewing ethics. Furthermore, high-involvement visitors preferred less developed settings for viewing wildlife and were much more likely to combine wildlife viewing with activities such as hiking, backpacking, cross-country skiing, and mountain climbing.

Roggenbuck, J. W.; Williams, D. R.; Watson, A. E. 1993. Defining acceptable conditions in wilderness. Environmental Management. 17(2):187-197.

Annotation: Visitors to four geographically diverse wilderness areas were surveyed to determine the best indicators of a quality wilderness experience. The results were then used to recommend potential indicators and standards for use in the Levels of Acceptable Change framework (see Stankey and others 1985). Among the 19 indicators on the questionnaire, the number of wild animals seen was consistently rated as one of the most important components of a quality wilderness experience. Although the authors recommend additional research to define acceptable standards for wildlife encounters, they express concern that managers have little control over the number of animals seen by a visitor. The authors state that several wilderness conditions, including wildlife encounters, are influenced more by visitor behavior than total visitor numbers. Thus, managers might better protect the wilderness resource by shaping visitor behavior than by limiting use.

Shafer, C. Scott; Hammitt, William E. 1994. Management conditions and indicators of importance in wilderness recreation experiences. In: Clonts, Howard H., ed. Proceedings of the 1993 Southeastern Recreation Research Conference: Volume 15. Gen. Tech. Rep. SE-90. Asheville, NC: U.S. Department of Agriculture, Forest Service, Southeastern Forest Experiment Station: 57-67.

Annotation: Visitors to Georgia's Cohutta Wilderness were surveyed to determine their concern for various wilderness conditions. Among the 35 conditions listed on the survey, both the number and the types of wildlife species seen were considered by visitors to be fairly important (among the 12 most valued conditions). The conditions were then grouped into six categories: human impact, natural features and processes, solitude, management confinement, primitive travel, and management-aided travel. After human impact conditions (litter, vegetation damage), "natural features and processes" was the second most important category. In addition to viewing wildlife, this category included the viewing of mature forests, naturally functioning ecosystems, and unusual plants.

Virden, Randy J.; Schreyer, Richard. 1988. Recreation specialization as an indicator of environmental preference. Environment and Behavior. 20(6):721-739.

Annotation: The authors surveyed hikers and backpackers at three Forest Service wilderness areas to determine if a wilderness user's degree of specialization affected their preferences for various physical, social, and managerial setting attributes. Degree of specialization was based on a hiker's experience level, economic commitment (in effect, amount of equipment owned), and the importance of hiking to their lifestyle. Of the 12 physical setting attributes, "seeing wildlife" was second most important to respondents, behind only "natural lakes and streams." This preference was universal among hikers of all skill levels. Respondents placed less importance on the "presence of bears," but more experienced hikers indicated a stronger preference for this attribute.

II. RECREATION IMPACTS ON WILDLIFE: GENERAL CONCEPTS

A. OVERVIEWS: RECREATION TRENDS AND IMPACTS

Although many backcountry recreational activities (for example, hiking, backpacking, camping, and nature photography) are often referred to as "nonconsumptive," these activities can impact natural resources such as wildlife (Wilkes 1977). Furthermore, the potential for these impacts has grown in recent years with the large increase in wilderness recreational use (Cole 1996), ecotourism (Buckley 2004a, b), and the significant growth of outdoor recreation in general (Cordell and Super 2000). Boyle and Samson (1985) summarize the wide variety of documented recreation impacts on wildlife. Knight and Cole (1995a) provide a more recent summary of documented impacts, as well as a conceptual model for understanding recreation impacts on wildlife. Many factors can influence the severity of these impacts, including traits of both the recreational activity and the affected wildlife (Knight and Cole 1995b).

Boyle, Stephen A.; Samson, Fred B. 1985. Effects of nonconsumptive recreation on wildlife: a review. Wildlife Society Bulletin. 13(2):110-116.

Annotation: The authors reviewed references containing original data on the effects of nonconsumptive recreation on wildlife. A total of 166 studies on recreational activities such as hiking and camping, wildlife observation and photography, spelunking, and rock climbing were reviewed. The most common study subjects were birds (61 percent), followed by mammals (42 percent) and reptiles and amphibians (4 percent). Negative effects on animal behavior, physiology, or distribution were reported in the large majority of cases for most activity types and all major taxa. A brief summary of the literature was provided for each recreational activity. The authors noted that previous research relied heavily on anecdotal observations. They discussed the need for more research using experimental approaches and quantitative assessments of long-term ecological effects.

Buckley, Ralf. 2004a. Impacts of ecotourism on terrestrial wildlife. In: Buckley, Ralf. ed. Environmental impacts of ecotourism. Ecotourism Series, No. 2. CABI Publishing; Wallingford, Oxfordshire, UK: 211-228.

Annotation: This book chapter reviews scientific literature on the disturbance of wildlife caused by outdoor recreation focused on nature and natural experiences. It provides an extensive list of articles on human recreation disturbance to mammals, reptiles, amphibians, and some invertebrates. Chapter sections focus on specific types of impacts including: habitat modifications, physiological disturbance (energetics), disturbance to breeding populations, habituation due to food and water provision, and the introduction of roadkill, light and noise pollution, and disease. The author also reviews behavioral changes resulting from disturbance such as avoidance behavior, alert and alarm behavior, evasive behavior, and aggressive behavior.

Buckley, Ralf. 2004b. Impacts of ecotourism on birds. In: Buckley, Ralf. ed. Environmental impacts of ecotourism. Ecotourism Series, No. 2. CABI Publishing; Wallingford, Oxfordshire, UK: 187-209.

Annotation: The author of this book chapter searched the database of the International Centre for Ecotourism Research at Griffith University for published literature on the impacts of ecotourism-related activities on birds. The extensive review includes definitions of ecotourism and activities related to ecotourism. Because relatively few articles refer to ecotourism specifically, the author includes most outdoor recreation activities and the wildlife impacts associated with these in his review, including vehicles, boats, and small scale infrastructure. Types of impacts covered are: modification of bird habitat, disturbance to adult birds (including both human activities and bird responses), energetic consequences of disturbance, and impacts on breeding bird populations.

Cole, David N. 1996. Wilderness recreation in the United States—trends in use, users, and impacts. International Journal of Wilderness. 2(3):14-18.

Annotation: Several long-term studies were synthesized to assess recreation trends within the National Wilderness Preservation System (NWPS). Recreational use of the original 54 U.S. Forest Service wilderness areas increased 86 percent between 1965 and 1994, and use was increasing throughout the NWPS. However, wilderness visitor characteristics, the types of trips taken, and the management preferences of visitors had not changed greatly in the prior 20 years. Although ecological impacts to trails and established campsites had been relatively stable over time, the number of campsites had increased greatly. For example, over a 15-year period in Oregon's Eagle Cap Wilderness, the number of campsites increased by 123 percent. The author discusses the shortcomings of current wilderness management efforts and provides management techniques for reducing campsite proliferation.

Cordell, H. Ken; Super, Gregory K. 2000. Trends in Americans' outdoor recreation. In: Gartner, William C.; Lime, David W., eds. Trends in outdoor recreation, leisure and tourism. Wallingford, United Kingdom: CABI Publishing: 133-144.

Annotation: By examining results from previous National Surveys on Recreation and the Environment (NSRE), the authors found that American participation in outdoor recreation activities increased greatly from 1960 to 1995. The number of participants in six outdoor recreation categories increased much more rapidly than the national population. Between 1983 and 1995, four of the five fastest-growing specific activities were bird watching, day hiking, backpacking, and primitive camping. The authors predict that new technologies and better access in upcoming years will facilitate further increases in outdoor recreation use and shift the demand to more isolated areas.

Hendee, John C.; Dawson, Chad P. 2002. Wilderness use and user trends. In: Hendee, John C.; Dawson, Chad P., eds. Wilderness management: stewardship and protection of resources and values. 3d ed. Golden, CO: Fulcrum Publishing: 373–411.

Annotation: See Section IV.B.2. Page 57.

Knight, Richard L.; Cole, David N. 1995a. Wildlife responses to recreationists. In: Knight, Richard L.; Gutzwiller, Kevin J., eds. Wildlife and recreationists: coexistence through management and research. Washington, DC: Island Press: 51-69.

Annotation: The authors present a conceptual model for understanding how recreation can impact wildlife. Indirect impacts result from habitat modification and pollution, and direct impacts occur due to exploitation and disturbance. Disturbance has short-term effects on wildlife behavior, but repeated disturbance can have long-term effects on individuals, populations, and communities. The authors also provide a brief literature review of recreation impacts on wildlife for a number of activities, including hunting, fishing, backpacking, hiking, cross-country skiing, horseback riding, rock climbing, spelunking, and boating. Finally, areas in need of further research are discussed, such as the energetic effects of disturbance, potential synergisms or interactions between recreational activities, and long-term effects on populations and communities.

Knight, Richard L.; Cole, David N. 1995b. Factors that influence wildlife responses to recreationists. In: Knight, Richard L.; Gutzwiller, Kevin J., eds. Wildlife and recreationists: coexistence through management and research. Washington, DC: Island Press: 71-79.

Annotation: Two types of factors influence the nature and severity of recreation impacts on wildlife: (1) characteristics of the recreational disturbance and (2) characteristics of the affected animals. Disturbance characteristics consist of activity type, recreationist's behavior, predictability, frequency, magnitude, timing, and location. Evidence suggests that rapid movements, direct approaches, and approaches from above elicit stronger responses from wildlife. Animal characteristics consist of animal type, group size, age, and sex. Comparative studies indicate that larger species and group sizes flush at greater distances than smaller species or group sizes. Disturbance frequency thresholds, above which impacts can occur, have been documented (for example, white-tailed deer movement in Missouri increased when hunting activity exceeded 0.45 hours per hectare). Although disturbance is often considered to be most detrimental during the breeding season, disturbance at other times of the year, such as winter, can have equally severe effects.

Knight, Richard L.; Gutzwiller, Kevin J., eds. 1995. Wildlife and recreationists: coexistence through management and research. Washington, DC: Island Press. 372 p.

Annotation: This book provides a comprehensive overview of recreation impacts on wildlife. Part I contains chapters on general issues such as outdoor recreation trends, management frameworks, and general concepts for understanding wildlife responses to recreation. Part II contains chapters summarizing more specific effects on wildlife physiology, populations, communities, and habitat. Part III contains a series of case studies including the effects of recreation on bald eagles in the Pacific Northwest, hunting on waterfowl, and beach recreation on nesting birds. Each chapter in the first three Parts concludes with sections on management options and research needs. Part IV contains a chapter reviewing general management options for reducing recreation impacts and concludes with a chapter on ethics.

Liddle, Michael. 1997. Recreation ecology: the ecological impact of outdoor recreation and ecotourism. London, United Kingdom: Chapman and Hall. 639 p.

Annotation: See section II.D. Page 22.

Newsome, David; Moore, Susan A.; Dowling, Ross K. 2002. Environmental impacts. In: Newsome, David; Moore, Susan A.; Dowling, Ross K. Natural area tourism: ecology, impacts and management. Clevedon, United Kingdom: Channel View Publications: 79-145.

Annotation: See section II.D. Page 23.

Wilkes, Brian. 1977. The myth of the non-consumptive user. Canadian Field-Naturalist. 91(4):343-349.

Annotation: The author rejects the concept that outdoor recreation activities such as hiking, backpacking, camping, and nature photography are nonconsumptive. In contrast, these activities consume spatial, visual, and physical resources. For example, "nonconsumptive" users trample vegetation, disturb wildlife, and distribute refuse across the landscape. Additional impacts result when facilities such as roads, parking lots, and campgrounds are built to provide access to natural areas for "nonconsumptive" users. Strict rules governing recreational behavior are called for, ranging from voluntary actions to government-mandated restrictions. According to Wilkes, the establishment of parks and other protected areas primarily to provide recreational opportunities for people should not be equated with land preservation, and some natural areas should be protected strictly for their ecological and existence values.

B. ASSESSING RECREATIONAL IMPACTS

Assessing the significance of recreational impacts on wildlife can be difficult. To prevent drawing erroneous conclusions from research studies, scientists must clearly articulate hypotheses and carefully design their studies, using an experimental approach whenever possible (Gutzwiller 1991, Hill and others 1997). Other factors that can influence wildlife behavior (for example, habitat features, weather, age and sex of animal) also need to be considered during study design, data collection, and statistical analyses (Gutzwiller 1991, Schueck and Marzluff 1995, Steidl and Powell 2006). Cumulative impacts, threshold levels, time lags, and interactions among disturbance variables should be considered and tested whenever feasible (Gutzwiller and Cole 2005, Harris 1988). This section also contains references with methods for collecting and analyzing data for potential recreation impacts (Blumstein and others 2005; Enggist-Düblin and Ingold 2003; Harris and others 1995b).

Blumstein, Daniel T.; Fernández-Juricic, Estaban; Zollner, Patrick A.; Garity, Susan C. 2005. Inter-specific variation in avian responses to human disturbance. Journal of Applied Ecology. 42:943-953.

Annotation: See section III.F. Page 41.

Enggist-Düblin, P., Ingold, P. 2003. Modelling the impact of different forms of wildlife harassment, exemplified by a quantitative comparison of the effects of hikers and paragliders on feeding and space use of chamois *Rupricapra rupricapra.* Wildlife Biology 9(1):37-45.

Annotation: The authors argue that repeated occurrence of recreational disturbance affects animals more than single disturbance events. They used several studies in the Swiss Alps to develop a model of the additive impacts of recreational disturbance on chamois (*Rupricapra rupricapra*). Their research on daily feeding activity was combined with data from other studies on chamois' reactions to hikers and paragliders. By quantifying measures of disturbance (for example, feeding interruption time and distance fled) that are additive, they created a model that computed amount of feeding time and area lost for each disturbance event. They then used this model to compare the two recreational disturbance types and predict impacts of increases in either recreation type. Their model predicted a much larger impact from paragliding on chamois than hiking. This difference was attributed to the reaction time in animals to each recreational type, and to the

fact that paragliders could affect animals anywhere in their range whereas hikers used trails almost exclusively. Thus, the area of hikers' impact was limited and the negative effects of hiking tapered with additional hikers as long as they remained on trails. The authors advocate using such models, which are easily adaptable to other species/recreation types, to understand subsequent biological and ecological effects of recreational disturbance and to predict the impacts of recreational disturbance before permanent damage occurs.

Gaines, William L.; Singleton, Peter H.; Ross, Roger C. 2003. Assessing the cumulative effects of linear recreation routes on wildlife habitats on the Okanogan and Wenatchee National Forests. U.S. Department of Agriculture, Forest Service, Pacific Northwest Research Station. Gen. Tech. Rep. PNW-GTR-586. 79 p.

Annotation: See section IV.B.3. Page 58.

Gill, Jennifer A. 2007. Approaches to measuring the effects of human disturbance on birds. Ibis. 149(Suppl. 1):9-14.

Annotation: Gill summarizes the approaches to studying human disturbance and wildlife according to three types of studies: 1) site-based approaches that investigate impacts on the numbers of animals using specific sites, 2) demographic approaches that assess reductions in survival or breeding success, and 3) population approaches that measure the density-dependent consequences of shifts in animal distributions due to disturbance. She provides examples of studies using each approach and describes the type of information each provides. Noting that behavioral responses depend on context and the trade-offs experienced by individuals, she explains that behavior cannot be reliably interpreted to assess vulnerability to human disturbance and that assessments of fitness consequences avoid this problem. Regarding the population approach, she explains that the density dependence of a species influences the extent to which redistributions of individuals impact population size. In fact, she concludes that "at a population scale any declines in survival or fecundity will result from density-dependence and not directly through disturbance," and that an understanding of density dependence must be taken into account when trying to maintain populations.

Gill, Jennifer A.; Sutherland, William J.; Watkinson, Andrew R. 1996. A method to quantify the effects of human disturbance on animal populations. Journal of Applied Ecology. 33:786-792.

Annotation: See section II.C.2. Page 19.

Gutzwiller, Kevin J. 1991. Assessing recreational impacts on wildlife: the value and design of experiments. Transactions of the North American Wildlife and Natural Resources Conference. 56:248-255.

Annotation: Although observational studies are usually more convenient and less expensive to conduct than experimental studies, field experiments are needed to establish cause-and-effect relationships between recreational activities and wildlife species. The author offers advice about how such experiments should be designed to maximize their interpretability. Researchers should: (1) ensure that experimental units are far enough apart in time and space to be independent, (2) use appropriate covariates (for example, habitat features, sex and age of animal) during data analysis to account for variation in the response variable, (3) consider testing for interaction effects among treatment types, and (4) use modified statistical tests when recreation treatments are expected to increase the variance of the response variable. In addition, researchers should consider biological factors that can influence the interpretation of results, such as potential time lags between disturbances and observed effects, an animal's ability to habituate to disturbance, its home range and territory size, and its responses to stimuli such as observer behavior or capture-and-handling.

Gutzwiller, Kevin J.; Cole, David N. 2005. Assessment and management of wildland recreational disturbance. In: Braun, Clait E., ed. Techniques for wildlife investigations and management. Sixth edition. The Wildlife Society: Bethesda, MD: 779-796.

Annotation: The authors of this chapter discuss methods for determining the nature and magnitude of recreational disturbances to wildlife and for reducing or avoiding these disturbances. Initially, managers can use existing information to identify species that require special consideration. For example, species with small home ranges and specific habitat requirements may be highly vulnerable to recreational activities in their habitat. The chapter includes recommendations for conducting field studies, both experimental and observational. In particular, managers and researchers are urged to consider possible complex effects from multiple disturbances, such as interactive, cumulative, ripple, threshold, and lag effects (see Harris 1998). The authors also discuss existing frameworks for managing recreational disturbances to wildlife (for example, Limits of Acceptable Change), elucidating the primary steps that most frameworks share in common. The chapter concludes with a review of strategies for achieving specified management goals—the manipulation of visitor characteristics, wildlife, and/or wildlife habitat.

Harris, Larry D. 1988. The nature of cumulative impacts on biotic diversity of wetland vertebrates. Environmental Management. 12(5):675-693.

Annotation: Cumulative impacts on biodiversity can result when a single impact occurs repeatedly or when a combination of different impacts occurs simultaneously. Although cumulative impacts are difficult to predict, case studies involving wetland vertebrates demonstrate the potential for these impacts to occur. For example, waterfowl, whose populations are generally declining, can be affected by hunting pressure in multiple locations (migratory staging areas, wintering areas) or by a combination of hunting, lead ingestion, and habitat loss. The effects of multiple factors can be additive or multiplicative, occur after a threshold is reached, occur after long time lags, or display a variety of

other complex interactions. Managers of protected areas must also take into account the surrounding landscape, especially when attempting to preserve large, wide-ranging species, interior-dependent species, and genetic integrity within species or populations.

Harris, Lisa K.; Gimblett, Randy H.; Shaw, William W. 1995b. Multiple use management: using a GIS model to understand conflicts between recreationists and sensitive wildlife. Society and Natural Resources. 8(6) 559-572.

Annotation: Using Geographical Information Systems (GIS) software, the authors identified locations where hikers may be encroaching upon mountain sheep (*Ovis canadensis mexicana*) habitat in Arizona's Pusch Ridge Wilderness. Based upon previous studies, sheep habitat was defined according to elevation, proximity to steep escape terrain, and radiotelemetry locations. The authors determined the spatial extent of recreational use by asking hikers how far they traveled along trails and whether and how far they traveled off-trail. Significant areas of overlap occurred between recreational use and sheep habitat, primarily because a large number of hikers traveled more than 400 m off-trail. The authors recommend GIS as a useful management tool for integrating large amounts of social and biological data.

Hill, David; Hockin, David; Price, David; Tucker, Graham; Morris, Rob; Treweek, Joanna. 1997. Bird disturbance: improving the quality and utility of disturbance research. Journal of Applied Ecology. 34(2):275-288.

Annotation: In the United Kingdom, reliable research of disturbance impacts on bird populations is needed due to: (1) increasing participation in activities such as water-based recreation, and (2) recent legislation mandating the protection of bird species. A review of the existing literature indicated that the majority of disturbance studies have been descriptive in nature and lacked formal hypothesis testing. Numerous suggestions are provided for future research at a local, regional, and flyway scale. For example, at the local scale, before-and-after experiments should be conducted at a range of sites. At the flyway scale, density-dependent population models should be developed and field tested. The authors provide three examples of what they deem to be high-quality research.

Pomerantz, Gerri A.; Decker, Daniel J.; Goff, Gary R.; Purdy, Ken G. 1988. Assessing impact of recreation on wildlife. Wildlife Society Bulletin. 16(1):58-62.

Annotation: Based on a phone survey of National Wildlife Refuge managers in the Northeast Region, the authors categorized recreational impacts on wildlife as follows: (1) direct mortality, (2) indirect mortality, (3) lowered productivity, (4) reduced use of a Refuge, (5) reduced use of preferred habitat, and (6) aberrant behavior or stress. In a later mail survey, 16 Refuge managers reported 148 impact situations involving 20 species. The most commonly reported impact was lowered productivity (41 percent of the cases). The authors suggest that this classification system will help all managers of multiple-use lands determine appropriate recreational uses and defend their management decisions.

Schueck, Linda S.; Marzluff, John M. 1995. **Influence of weather on conclusions about effects of human activities on raptors.** Journal of Wildlife Management. 59(4):674-682.

Annotations: When assessing disturbance impacts on wildlife, research conclusions can be greatly influenced by the failure to account for uncontrollable abiotic factors such as weather. In a study of the effects of military activity on raptor abundance, the authors reversed several of their initial conclusions after including wind speed and temperature as covariates in their statistical analysis. Furthermore, analyses that included weather covariates explained 30 percent of the observed variation in raptor abundance, compared to only 3 percent when weather covariates were not included. Because weather often affects animal behavior, the authors recommend that researchers collect and appropriately analyze weather data during behavioral studies.

Steidl, Robert J; Powell, Brian F. 2006. **Assessing the effects of human activities on wildlife.** George Wright Forum. 23(2):50-58.

Annotation: Focusing on short duration recreational activities (for example, hiking, wildlife viewing, boating), which can have short- or long-term effects, Steidl and Powell provide a conceptual framework for assessing the effects of human activities on wildlife. They recommend that study objectives clearly specify the human activity; the timing, intensity, and spatial extent of the activity; the focal wildlife species; and the range of potential responses. They differentiate between research and monitoring, noting that research is designed to address specific resource management questions whereas monitoring quantifies resource changes over time. Most of this paper discusses the appropriate wildlife response measures for short- versus long-term studies, as well as the implications of drawing conclusions based on inappropriate response measures.

Sutherland, William J. 2007. **Future directions in disturbance research.** Ibis. 149(Suppl. 1):120-124.

Annotation: Sutherland recommends 12 research questions to further understanding of human disturbance to wildlife: what determines patterns of human disturbance; how can we determine population-level responses to disturbance; are there general rules for predicting how important disturbance will be; how important are disturbance-derived ecological traps; what is the interaction between predation and disturbance; when does habituation occur; how do physiological responses to disturbance affect population size; what is the evidence for changes in access impacting upon populations; what are the positive consequences of access to the countryside; how important is habitat specific disturbance; which measures reduce human impact and how can large-scale planning minimize the impact of disturbance? In conclusion, he predicts a change from research that shows disturbance impacts to research on the most effective means of mitigation and visitor control in order to identify precise management problems and solutions.

C. DIRECT IMPACTS OF RECREATION ON WILDLIFE

Recreation can potentially impact wildlife on three levels—individual, population, and community. Most studies have measured individual responses to disturbance. If an activity elicits a significant behavioral response from individuals, occurs frequently, and/or is widespread, long-term impacts to the reproduction and survival of individuals is possible. In the first section, Whittaker and Knight (1998) review the different types of behavioral response, while Gabrielsen and Smith (1995) review potential physiological responses. In addition, Frid and Dill (2002) provide a theoretical framework for predicting and interpreting behavioral responses, while Wingfield and Ramenofsky (1999) provide a theoretical model for understanding the long-term physiological effects of disturbance. Although motorized vehicles are generally prohibited in wilderness, aircraft and snowmobile use (both legal and illegal) is common in some wilderness areas and National Parks. Thus, we include overviews of wildlife responses to noise (Bowles 1995) and aircraft (USDI National Park Service 1995).

If a large enough number of individuals is negatively affected by recreation, impacts at the population level can occur. Furthermore, if impacted wildlife populations have important interactions with other species, community impacts are also possible. The assessment of population and community impacts has been rare, mainly due to the enormous effort and time required to conduct such studies and the difficulty in controlling for confounding factors. In the second and third sections, potential population and community responses to disturbance are reviewed. Riffell and others (1996) provide a notable example of a long-term experimental study of an avian community. Researchers must often rely on comparative studies between different populations or within the same population at different times (Green 1994). In addition, population and community effects are sometimes extrapolated from behavioral observations (Gill and others 1996; Goss-Custard and others 1994; Skagen and others 1991). Such extrapolations require caution, however, because the magnitude of a behavioral response is not necessarily related to its impact on a wildlife population (Gill and others 2001a).

1. Behavioral and Physiological Responses

Bowles, Ann E. 1995. **Responses of wildlife to noise.** In: Knight, Richard L.; Gutzwiller, Kevin J., eds. Wildlife and recreationists: coexistence through management and research. Washington, DC: Island Press: 109-156.

Annotation: The author defines noise as "any human-made sound that alters the behavior of animals or interferes with their normal functioning." Sound travel is affected by sound properties such as frequency and by a host of environmental factors including temperature, humidity, wind, and vegetation. Although human noise is not generally intense or constant enough in wilderness areas to damage the auditory systems of wildlife, chronic exposure to noise can result in physiological effects such as elevated stress hormone levels, reproductive failure, and increased energy use. Behavioral effects include changes in habitat use, increased exposure to predators, and reduced parental care. Numerous examples of observed physiological and behavioral effects are provided from the literature. Management recommendations, such as making noise sources more predictable in time and space, are provided to reduce noise impacts on wildlife.

Frid, Alejandro; Dill, Lawrence. 2002. Human-caused disturbance stimuli as a form of predation risk. Conservation Ecology. 6(1):11. *(Note: This journal, renamed Ecology and Society, is only available online at http://www.consecol.org [April 18, 2008].)*

Annotation: The authors assert that wildlife responses to human disturbance stimuli are analogous to anti-predatory behavior. Thus, animals should optimize their response by balancing avoidance costs with the perceived predation risk presented by the stimuli. Based on this theoretical framework, specific predictions of wildlife responses to human disturbance can be made. For example, animals should be more likely to flee when approached more directly, more quickly, or by larger group sizes, or when the costs of fleeing are lower. Fleeing costs might be lower if the current resource patch is poor, rich resources are evenly distributed and easily found elsewhere, or environmental conditions are mild. The authors reviewed existing disturbance literature to test predictions based on the predation-risk hypothesis, and found that the large majority of examples supported the hypothesis. They note the effects of human disturbance on mate acquisition and parental investment warrant further research. The authors suggest that applying this theory to study design and analysis will result in more focused research and improve our understanding of the variability in wildlife responses to disturbance.

Gabrielsen, Geir Wing; Smith, E. Norbert. 1995. Physiological responses of wildlife to disturbance. In: Knight, Richard L.; Gutzwiller, Kevin J., eds. Wildlife and recreationists: coexistence through management and research. Washington, DC: Island Press: 95-107.

Annotation: Wildlife can physiologically respond to disturbance in two ways. During the active defense response, the animal moves away from the source of disturbance. This response is accompanied by increased heart rate, blood sugar level, and respiration, and decreased food digestion. During the passive defense response, the animal remains motionless and the physiological effects are opposite to those of the active defense response. There are two critical periods when many species are most sensitive to human disturbance: the immediate postnatal period in mammals and the breeding period in birds. During these periods, human disturbance should be minimized. Studies have generally shown that birds and mammals are more tolerant of mechanical noise and vehicles than the presence of humans on foot. In sensitive areas, the authors recommend that hikers be confined to definite paths or access restricted to certain times of the year.

U.S. Department of the Interior, National Park Service. 1995. Effects of overflights on wildlife. In: Report on effects of aircraft overflights on the National Park System. Washington, DC: U.S. Department of the Interior, National Park Service: 103-130.

Annotation: Two types of aircraft activity occur in backcountry areas: (1) low-altitude overflights by military aircraft and (2) airplane and helicopter overflights related to tourism and resource extraction. The authors summarize the existing literature for aircraft effects on wildlife, noting that a disproportionate number of studies have concentrated on ungulates and certain bird species. A wide range of behavioral and physiological responses have been detected, depending on the species and individual. Factors such as an animal's physiological status, terrain, aircraft type, and flight frequency can influence animal responses to aircraft. Qualitative criteria are presented to guide management efforts in situations where aircraft impacts on wildlife may be occurring.

Whittaker, Doug; Knight, Richard L. 1998. Understanding wildlife responses to humans. Wildlife Society Bulletin. 26(2):312-317.

Annotation: Animals can find human-provided stimuli to be reinforcing (leading to attraction), aversive (leading to avoidance), or neutral (leading to habituation). The authors stress that the term "habituation" is often misused and confused with "attraction." These responses can be linked. For example, habituation may lead to attraction because habituated wildlife has greater opportunity to encounter attractive human stimuli. The current emphasis on observational studies makes it difficult to assess behavioral causes, but past research suggests that genetic and learned components are both involved and may be interrelated. Further, an individual's behavioral tendency is sometimes labeled based on a few limited responses, or a population is labeled based on the responses of a few individuals. These extrapolations extend beyond observed events and should be made cautiously. Finally, value judgments are commonly attached to behavioral responses (for example, habituation is either good or bad), but these judgments are often overly simplistic. For example, habituated bears may be more likely to avoid conflict with recreationists but also more likely to be killed by hunters.

Wingfield, John C.; Ramenofsky, Marilyn. 1999. Hormones and the behavioral ecology of stress. In: Balm, Paul H. M., ed. Stress physiology in animals. Sheffield, United Kingdom: Sheffield Academic Press: 1-51.

Annotation: Unpredictable events in an animal's environment can trigger a physiological stress response by stimulating the secretion of stress hormones called glucocorticosteroids (also known as glucocorticoids). Among other effects, glucocorticoids promote the metabolism of energy reserves. The authors suggest that prolonged or chronic stressors (for example, recreational disturbances) can result in an energy deficit for an individual, prompting an "emergency life history stage" (ELHS). During an

ELHS, an animal may postpone or abandon its normal current life history stage (for example, reproduction) until a positive energy balance can be restored. Factors that can affect this response, such as individual variation, habitat type, and body condition, are discussed and numerous examples from the literature are given.

2. Projected Population Responses

Anderson, Stanley H. 1995. Recreational disturbance and wildlife populations. In: Knight, Richard L.; Gutzwiller, Kevin J., eds. Wildlife and recreationists: coexistence through management and research. Washington, DC: Island Press: 157-168.

Annotation: Recreation can impact wildlife populations by displacing wildlife from otherwise suitable habitat, increasing exposure to predators, disrupting reproduction or parental care of offspring, elevating wildlife stress levels, and increasing wildlife energy expenditures. However, few studies have documented population-level effects. Recreation impacts can vary according to an animal's sex or life history stage. Thus, the author recommends construction of a life table to estimate population-level effects and identify sensitive periods during an animal's lifespan. To minimize impacts on wildlife populations, the author suggests closing or restricting access to critical habitats and providing visitor education on practices that minimize recreation impact.

Drewitt, Allan L. 2007. Birds and recreational disturbance. Ibis. 149(Suppl. 1):1-2.

Annotation: Following the 2000 Countryside and Rights of Way Act in England and Wales, English Nature commissioned an assessment of research needs for birds and recreational access. Key researchers agreed that the objectives should be to "increase the understanding of how disturbance can affect bird populations and identify solutions." Research was commissioned specifically to address the application of population models, further develop behavior-based individual energetic models to predict the effect of disturbance on non-breeding birds, and to quantify disturbance effects in terms of resource use. This paper provides an introduction to the proceedings of the 2005 British Ornithologists' Union Autumn Scientific Meeting on Birds and Recreational Disturbance, where results of work on these topics were presented. The proceedings were published in the journal Ibis 149(Supplement 1).

Gill, Jennifer A. 2007. Approaches to measuring the effects of human disturbance on birds. Ibis. 149(Suppl. 1):9-14.

Annotation: See section II.B. Page 15.

Gill, Jennifer A.; Sutherland, William J.; Watkinson, Andrew R. 1996. A method to quantify the effects of human disturbance on animal populations. Journal of Applied Ecology. 33:786-792.

Annotation: The authors quantified the effects of disturbance on a pink-footed goose (*Anser brachyrhynchus*)

population based on the amount of food left uneaten by wintering geese. The geese fed on crop waste in agricultural fields during the day. Birds feeding closer to a road were more easily disturbed. Furthermore, the proportion of grain left uneaten in a field was correlated with initial flock proximity to a road. Disturbance impacts to the population were then estimated by converting the biomass of unused food into the number of additional birds that could have been supported. This approach is applicable to other animal species, forms of disturbance, and types of limiting resources (for example, nest or roost sites).

Gill, Jennifer A.; Norris, Ken; Sutherland, William J. 2001a. Why behavioural responses may not reflect the population consequences of human disturbance. Biological Conservation. 97(2):265-268.

Annotation: Species that show a strong behavioral response to humans are often considered to be in greater need of protection from disturbance than those that do not. However, the authors argue that the degree of response is not always a good indication of potential population-level effects. The decision of whether or not to move away from a disturbed site will be influenced by factors such as the quality of the occupied site, distance to and quality of alternate sites, and investment that an individual has made in the occupied site (for example, territory establishment). Thus, animals with no suitable habitat nearby may be forced to remain in an area of intense disturbance, even if there is a large fitness cost in terms of reduced survival or fecundity. Conversely, if many alternative sites are available, animals may move in response to a small degree of disturbance. To adequately assess disturbance impacts to a population, future studies should address how behavioral responses affect demographic parameters.

Goss-Custard, John D.; Caldow, Richard W.G.; Clarke, Ralph T.; Durell, Sarah E.A. le V. dit; Urfi, Jamil; West, Andy D. 1994. Consequences of habitat loss and change to populations of wintering migratory birds: predicting the local and global effects from studies of individuals. Ibis. 137:S56-S66.

Annotation: The authors present an individuals-based, density-dependent model that predicts winter mortality of oystercatchers (*Haematopus ostralegus*). As habitat is lost (for example, due to disturbance), population density is expected to rise, thereby reducing an individual's ability to obtain food and leading to increased mortality rates. Model parameters include susceptibility to interference from conspecifics, average food abundance, and individual variation in foraging efficiency. These parameters can be estimated by field observations. Using similar behavioral and ecological parameters, this general approach may be used to predict the effects of habitat loss on other animal species.

Goss-Custard, John D.; Sutherland, William J. 1997. Individual behavior, populations, and conservation. In: Krebs, John R.; Davies, Nicholas B., eds. Behaviorial ecology: an evolutionary approach. Oxford, UK: Blackwell Publishing: 373-395.

Annotation: This chapter demonstrates how behavioral studies can be used to predict demographic functions for population modeling. This approach assumes that individual choices are based on decision principles, such as optimization, that are unlikely to change even though exact choices that affect survival and reproduction do change. The authors describe the importance of density dependence to population biology, illustrate how to estimate the strength of density dependence, and explain how these functions may change as a result of habitat loss or change. The authors address the tradeoffs between detailed ecological models and general simplified models, and they recommend using behavioral ecological models to derive decision rules that can be used in models designed to predict population consequences.

Green, R. E. 1994. Diagnosing causes of bird population declines. Ibis. 137:S47-S55.

Annotation: To identify the factors responsible for bird population declines, researchers often compare populations from different geographic areas or time periods because other methods may be impractical. For example, manipulative field experiments may need to be conducted on a large scale, making it difficult to obtain a desirable number of replicate experimental and control plots. Simulation modeling requires considerable time and resources to develop and validate. Although practical, using the comparative approach requires caution because conclusions are based on observed correlations rather than demonstrated relationships. Therefore, the author recommends that those using this approach consider: (1) all plausible agents of decline and their effects on breeding success or survival, (2) evidence of movements between geographic areas, and (3) the use of manipulative experiments whenever possible.

Liley, Durwyn; Sutherland, William J. 2007. Predicting the population consequences of human disturbance for Ringed Plovers *Charadrius hiaticula*: a game theory approach. Ibis. 149(Suppl. 1):82-94.

Annotation: This paper describes a model used to predict the population consequences of human disturbance to breeding birds. Three seasons of breeding data and habitat variables representing quality were used to predict breeding success, site occupancy, and the number of plover pairs for a given area. The authors then predicted an equilibrium population size for the study area based on known density-independent adult winter mortality, predicted density-dependent breeding success, and habitat variables. They compared the effects of 11 disturbance scenarios on equilibrium population size. The models showed large variations in predicted population size based on different disturbance levels. The authors explain that density-dependence influences territorial behavior through three mechanisms: larger population size leads to smaller territories, larger population size leads to the use of poorer quality sites, or individuals do not breed. They suggest this approach can be used for almost any species.

Mallord, John. W.; Dolman, Paul M.; Brown, Andy F.; Sutherland, William J. 2007. Linking recreational disturbance to population size in a ground-nesting passerine. Journal of Applied Ecology. 44:185-195.

Annotation: Studying woodlarks (*Lullula arborea*) in southern England's heathland habitats, the authors present a model used to predict population consequences across a range of recreation access scenarios. Model results showed that both numbers of people and their spatial distribution were important predictors of woodlark productivity. The authors also present a habitat suitability model and summarize the potential effects of disturbance on woodlark distribution, nest survival, and productivity. They note that behavioral studies can be misleading in terms of which species are most vulnerable to disturbance and emphasize that population consequences must be used to assess the severity of recreation access threats.

Reed, J. Michael; Mills, L. Scott; Dunning, John B., Jr.; Menges, Eric S.; McKelvey, Kevin S.; Frye, Robert; Beissinger, Steven R.; Anstett, Marie-Charlotte; Miller, Philip. 2002. Emerging issues in population viability analysis. Conservation Biology. 16(1):7-19.

Annotation: Population viability analysis (PVA) may be used to assess the relative effects of potential management actions on population growth or persistence. As PVA models become more complex and PVA software becomes more available, a greater potential exists for misinterpretation of model results. The authors review the development of spatially explicit models, use of sensitivity analyses to identify the factors that most affect population growth, and incorporation of genetic effects into models. They also caution that models should be treated as hypotheses to be tested, results should be presented with an appropriate assessment of confidence, and more research should examine density-dependent changes in population parameters.

Ruggiero, Leonard F.; Hayward, Gregory D.; Squires, John R. 1994. Viability analysis in biological evaluations: concepts of population viability analysis, biological population, and ecological scale. Conservation Biology. 8(2):364-372.

Annotation: When conducting environmental impact assessments, managers often consider the impacts of proposed management actions on the viability of animal populations. These efforts usually involve a gross mismatch of scale, however, as managers consider the impacts of local management actions on a geographically extensive ecological response (species persistence). For a more meaningful analysis, the authors propose that managers either consider a greater number of management actions together over a large area or consider the impacts of local actions on a smaller biological unit (for example, local population). The authors also offer guidelines for conducting a population viability assessment. For example, local population ranges of some species are still much larger than the area affected by local management forest actions. In these cases, managers should either delineate a larger area for analysis (for example, a National Forest Ranger District) or assess the impacts of management actions on individuals rather than populations. When faced with making a final evaluation based on limited information, managers can use general ecological principles to support their decision (for example, species with low reproductive rates are more sensitive than species with high reproductive rates).

3. Projected Community Responses

Cole, David N.; Knight, Richard L. 1990. Impacts of recreation on biodiversity in wilderness. In: Wilderness areas: their impacts; proceedings of a symposium; 1990 April 19–20; Logan, UT. Logan, UT: Utah State University: 33-40.

Annotation: Wilderness recreational use can impact biodiversity at many levels. For example, genetic diversity is affected by the selective hunting of dominant individuals or by hybridization with stocked nonnative fish. Across the entire National Wilderness Preservation System, the authors suggest that hunting and fishing are the recreational activities having the greatest effect on wilderness biodiversity. Although recreation can affect the species diversity and composition of communities, these impacts are usually only locally significant. However, if keystone mammal or bird species are displaced from large areas, broad-scale changes in diversity are possible. Although studies of long-term or widespread impacts are lacking, recreational use in 1990 was not thought to be the primary threat to wilderness biodiversity. Rather, fire management policies, nonconforming uses, and external threats were considered to be more serious factors affecting wilderness biodiversity.

Gutzwiller, Kevin J. 1995. Recreational disturbance and wildlife communities. In: Knight, Richard L.; Gutzwiller, Kevin J., eds. Wildlife and recreationists: coexistence through management and research. Washington, DC: Island Press: 169-181.

Annotation: Although it has rarely been documented, recreationists can theoretically impact communities by: (1) altering competitive, facilitative, and predator-prey interactions between species and (2) altering species richness and abundance. These impacts can occur due to displacement of wildlife from habitat and/or alteration of habitat structure. To minimize wildlife displacement by recreationists, management recommendations include establishing buffer zones, reducing activities in critical habitats, or restricting access during crucial periods of a species' annual cycle. In areas where habitat structure has been impacted, closure and restoration is recommended. Future research investigating recreation impacts on community structure, stability, and restoration, as well as potential cumulative or synergistic effects of different recreational activities, is recommended.

Riffell, Samuel K.; Gutzwiller, Kevin J.; Anderson, Stanley H. 1996. Does repeated human intrusion cause cumulative declines in avian richness and abundance? Ecological Applications. 6(2):492-505.

Annotation: An experimental approach was used to test for effects of human intrusion on an avian community in mixed-conifer forest in Wyoming. Over a period of 5 years, solitary hikers intruded upon experimental plots for 1 to 2 hours each week for 10 consecutive weeks during the breeding season. Seasonal species richness and abundances for all species, groups of common and uncommon species, and six guilds were then compared between experimental and nearby control plots. Relative richness and abundance for the group of common species were the only metrics to exhibit significant declines during some years, and these declines were not cumulative. Cumulative declines may not have been observed due to replacement of displaced individuals by birds from the surrounding area or a developed tolerance to the intrusions by breeding birds. At least with the avian guilds observed, these results illustrate that unwarranted extrapolation of an effect over time may lead to inaccurate predictions of long-term impacts and management decisions that unnecessarily restrict recreational use.

Skagen, Susan K.; Knight, Richard L.; Orians, Gordon H. 1991. Human disturbance of an avian scavenging guild. Ecological Applications. 1(2):215-225.

Annotation: This study measured the behavioral responses of bald eagles (*Haliaeetus leucocephalus*), American crows (*Corvus brachyrhynchos*), and glaucous-winged gulls (*Larus glaucescens*) to human disturbance using both observational data and experiments. On days with disturbance, the proportion of salmon (*Oncorhynchus* spp.) eaten by eagles was significantly reduced, from 55 percent of the total consumed to 6 percent. Gulls are competitively inferior to eagles but tolerate closer approach by recreationists. Thus, gull foraging success at carcasses quadrupled when eagles were flushed from carcasses. The authors suggest that reductions in eagle numbers due to disturbance may eventually reduce foraging opportunities for crows and gulls because eagles open carcasses for these secondary scavengers. While this study did not assess population-level effects, the authors suggest that disturbance could ultimately affect the composition of this avian scavenging guild.

D. INDIRECT IMPACTS OF RECREATION ON WILDLIFE HABITAT

Recreation can indirectly impact wildlife by altering soils, plants, and water (Cole and Landres 1995). An extensive amount of research exists on this topic with a particular emphasis on campsite and trail impacts. Rather than attempt to select specific studies from the literature, we provide a small number of comprehensive general references on the subject, which can be used to locate more specific references.

However, a specific study on rock-climbing impacts on plant communities is included (McMillan and Larson 2002) because such studies are rare.

Recreation impacts on plants largely result from trampling, which reduces plant cover, height, and biomass (Hammitt 1986). Most vegetation damage occurs quickly at low and moderate levels of visitor use and levels off with increasing use (Leung and Marion 2000). Plant species vary in their resistance to trampling, leading to changes in plant communities. In general, plant diversity has been shown to increase with slight use and to decrease as use intensifies (Liddle 1997). Wilderness areas are often located in alpine, arctic, and desert ecosystems where abiotic factors limit plant growth. Plant recovery from trampling damage in these areas can take many years and may never occur (Newsome and others 2002).

Recreation impacts on soils also result primarily from trampling. Trampling loosens the soil's surface layers but compacts the underlying layers. Coupled with a loss of plant cover, this leads to increased soil erosion (Hammitt 1986). Trampling also decreases the abundance and diversity of soil organisms such as microbes, earthworms, arthropods, snails, and slugs, which often play a major role in nutrient cycling (Liddle 1997). Again, wilderness areas are often located in ecosystems where soil formation to replace lost soil is slow. In addition, desert environments frequently have biological soil crusts, which play a significant role in ecosystem processes and are particularly susceptible to damage (Newsome and others 2002).

Cole, David N.; Landres, Peter B. 1995. Indirect effects of recreationists on wildlife. In: Knight, Richard L.; Gutzwiller, Kevin J., eds. Wildlife and recreationists: coexistence through management and research. Washington, DC: Island Press: 183-202.

Annotation: Recreational impacts on soil, vegetation, and aquatic systems can change animal habitat. However, indirect impacts are more poorly understood than direct impacts, largely because of the lack of interest in animal species that are most affected (many invertebrates). Habitat changes resulting from recreation can affect animals by altering the availability of food or living space. The authors provide many examples from the existing literature. In contrast to direct impacts, many indirect impacts are long-lasting and occur only after a time lag. Thus, regulating the seasonal timing of recreational activities is less effective at reducing these impacts. Viable management options include restricting the amount, type, and spatial distribution of use and enhancing site durability. Although indirect impacts are often localized, they can be significant if they are extensive and severe, affect rare or important habitat, or affect rare or keystone species.

Hammitt, William E. 1986. Resource impacts of recreation on wilderness. In: Kulhavy, David L.; Conner, Richard N., eds. Wilderness and natural areas in the eastern United States: a management challenge. Nacogdoches, TX: Center for Applied Studies, School of Forestry, Stephen F. Austin State University: 253-258.

Annotation: This paper begins with a review of the mechanisms by which recreation impacts the soil, vegetation, and water. Several studies are cited in which impacts occur rapidly with recreational use whereas site recovery takes considerably longer. Within a given wilderness area, there exist a variety of habitats and zones differing in their sensitivity to recreational impacts. The author recommends that these zones be mapped within natural areas and recreational use be encouraged in areas that are more resistant to impact.

Leung, Yu-Fai; Marion, Jeffrey L. 2000. Recreation impacts and management in wilderness: a state-of-knowledge review. In: Cole, David N.; McCool, Stephen F.; Borrie, William T.; O'Loughlin, Jennifer, comps. Wilderness science in a time of change conference—Volume 5: Wilderness ecosystems, threats, and management; 1999 May 23–27; Missoula, MT. Proceedings RMRS-P-15-VOL-5. Ogden, UT: U.S. Department of Agriculture, Forest Service, Rocky Mountain Research Station: 23-48.

Annotation: The authors reviewed the literature on recreation impacts and management, primarily focusing on research conducted within designated wilderness during the previous 15 years. Previous recreation impact study designs and techniques were reviewed. Four common study designs, in order of increasing ability to infer cause-and-effect, were: (1) descriptive surveys, (2) comparison of used and unused sites, (3) before-and-after natural experiments, and (4) before-and-after simulated experiments. Research has investigated the impacts of trails, camping, packstock grazing, climbing, and human waste and the effectiveness of specific management strategies. Management of use-related factors, particularly the redistribution or limitation of visitor use, has received the greatest research and management attention. However, the authors note the curvilinear use-impact relationship limits the potential effectiveness of visitor restrictions. Research has increasingly demonstrated the importance of focusing use in environmentally resistant locations.

Liddle, Michael. 1997. Recreation ecology: the ecological impact of outdoor recreation and ecotourism. London, United Kingdom: Chapman and Hall. 639 p.

Annotation: In this textbook, the author provides an overview of ecological impacts resulting from all types of outdoor recreation. Six chapters discuss impacts on plants, eight chapters discuss soil impacts, and 11 chapters discuss human disturbance of wildlife. Wildlife chapters are organized by taxonomic groups including invertebrates, reptiles, birds, fish, aquatic mammals, bears, and deer. Wildlife responses to a range of recreational activities are reviewed, including hunting, fishing, vehicle use, hiking, and camping. An overview chapter on disturbance defines three levels of disturbance based on the severity of impacts on wildlife, and a table is provided which subjectively rates the degree to which 29 different recreational activities can cause each of the three levels of disturbance.

McMillan, Michelle A.; Larson, Douglas W. 2002. Effects of rock climbing on the vegetation of the Niagara Escarpment in southern Ontario, Canada. Conservation Biology. 16(2):389-398.

Annotation: The authors examined rock-climbing effects on the vascular plant, bryophyte, and lichen communities along the Niagara Escarpment in southern Ontario. Abundance and species richness of vascular plants and bryophytes were significantly lower in climbed areas than in unclimbed areas. Lichen abundance was the same on climbed and unclimbed cliffs, but species richness was significantly lower in climbed areas. In addition, the proportion of alien plants was three times higher in climbed areas. Managers were advised to prohibit the establishment of new climbing routes in the area and to conduct a long-term study monitoring the recovery of cliff plants after the removal of climbing pressure.

Newsome, David; Moore, Susan A.; Dowling, Ross K. 2002. Environmental impacts. In: Newsome, David; Moore, Susan A.; Dowling, Ross K. Natural area tourism: ecology, impacts and management. Clevedon, United Kingdom: Channel View Publications: 79-145.

Annotation: This chapter reviews the environmental impacts associated with tourism and recreational activities such as boating, off-road vehicles, hiking, camping, horse riding, and caving. A section on trampling reviews impacts on vegetation, biological crusts, and soils. Other sections review impacts associated with access roads and trails, buildings and campgrounds, and activities that are concentrated along riverbanks, lakeshores, and coastal areas. A section on wildlife observation discusses traits that make certain species particularly vulnerable to approach by humans and the types of behavioral responses that occur.

III. Recreation Impacts on Wildlife: Specific Examples

A. CARNIVORES

Bear responses to recreational use are often studied because of the potential for injury or harm to humans and bears. Documented bear responses include the avoidance of suitable habitat near trails and campsites (Kasworm and Manley 1990, Mace and Waller 1996), attraction to campsites and human foods that can lead to the extermination of "problem" bears (Graber 1986; Merrill 1978; Pitt and Jordan 1996), and energetically costly movements within and out of winter dens (Goodrich and Berger 1994, Linnell and others 2000). Bear responses can vary depending on a bear's previous experience with humans and the characteristics of the recreationists (Albert and Bowyer 1991; Jope 1984; McLellan and Shackleton 1989). Recreation impact studies on carnivores other than bears are rare, but references are included for the gray wolf (*Canis lupus*), Florida panther (*Puma concolor coryi*), mountain lion (*Felis concolor*), and lynx (*Lynx lynx*).

1. Bears

Albert, David M.; Bowyer, R. Terry. 1991. Factors related to grizzly bear-human interactions in Denali National Park. Wildlife Society Bulletin. 19(3):339-349.

Annotation: The authors collected information on interactions (either an incident or encounter) between grizzly bears (*Ursus arctos*) and Park visitors during two consecutive summers. A total of 203 interactions were recorded, 19 of which involved bear aggression toward humans. Human group sizes were significantly smaller in cases of bear aggression than in cases where bears displayed inquisitive or avoidance behavior. Interactions occurred more frequently than expected on river and gravel bars, which are used as travel corridors by bears and people. Frontcountry interactions were high in May and early June, whereas backcountry interactions were high in July and August. The authors hypothesize that nonhabituated bears were displaced into backcountry areas as human activity increased in the frontcountry.

Aumiller, Larry D.; Matt, Colleen A. 1994. Management of McNeil River State Game Sanctuary for viewing of brown bears. International Conference on Bear Research and Management. 9(1):51-61.

Annotation: See section IV.B.4. Page 60.

Bromley, Marianne, ed. 1989. Bear-people conflicts: proceedings of a symposium on management strategies; 1987 April 6–10; Yellowknife, Northwest Territories. Yellowknife, Northwest Territories: Northwest Territories Department of Renewable Resources. 246 p.

Annotation: This proceedings contains 34 research papers pertaining to the management of bear-human conflict. Research on all three North American bear species (grizzly, black, and polar) is included. Section I contains papers about the behavior and ecology of problem bears with an emphasis on habituation and the consequences of bears obtaining human foods. Section II discusses several bear detection and deterrent techniques. Section III is the largest section and presents case studies of various bear management programs throughout North America. Section IV includes a paper on public education efforts and a paper on strategies to improve communication between scientists and the media.

Chi, Danielle K.; Gilbert, Barrie K. 1999. Habitat security for Alaskan black bears at key foraging sites: are there thresholds for human disturbance? Ursus. 11:225-238.

Annotation: Black bear (*Ursus americanus*) feeding activity was assessed at an Alaskan salmon (*Onchorhynchus* spp.) stream in relation to human activity on an adjacent viewing platform. The viewing site was located at the lower falls, and the upper falls (control site) were closed to the public. The upper falls received considerably more bear use, possibly to avoid human activity, but the fishing opportunities were also greater at the upper falls. Adult males dominated the upper falls area, displacing females with cubs to the lower falls. Bears at the lower falls were tolerant of humans, and the number of bears using the lower falls was not related to visitor numbers. However, the amount of time spent on each foraging bout decreased as visitor numbers increased. All foraging bouts of 15 minutes or longer occurred when fewer than 10 people were on the platform, suggesting a possible disturbance threshold.

Goodrich, John M.; Berger, Joel. 1994. Winter recreation and hibernating black bears *Ursus americanus*. Biological Conservation. 67(2):105-110.

Annotation: In California and Nevada, the authors documented several instances of winter den abandonment by black bears (*Ursus americanus*) due to investigator disturbance. Den abandonment could adversely affect the reproductive success and physical condition of bears. In two cases, females abandoned new-born cubs when researchers approached a den. Although den abandonment due to recreational disturbance was not documented, it may occur on the Lake Tahoe portion of the study area where winter recreation use is heavy. In addition, bear den sites and ski runs are often both located on northeast-facing slopes, where snow accumulation is greatest.

Graber, David M. 1986. Conflicts between wilderness users and black bears in the Sierra Nevada National Parks. In: Lucas, Robert C., ed. Proceedings—national wilderness research conference: current research; 1985 July 23–26. Ogden, UT: U.S. Department of Agriculture, Forest Service, Intermountain Research Station: 197-202.

Annotation: Conflicts between black bears (*Ursus americanus*) and wilderness users in Yosemite and Kings Canyon National Parks are a serious management concern. Backcountry campsites in these parks represent a concentrated, low-risk food source for bears. During this century, the bear population has expanded into high-elevation areas in response to increased backcountry camping. A survey of backcountry campers in Yosemite found that 95 percent had received a brochure about proper food storage and 92 percent reported that their food was protected, but only 3 percent were properly storing their food. The pros and cons of various bear management options are reviewed. The author advocates the use of portable bear-proof food canisters rather than cables, poles, and food lockers because of their minimal impact on wilderness values.

Jope, Katherine; Shelby, Bo. 1984. Hiker behavior and the outcome of interactions with grizzly bears. Leisure Sciences. 6(3):257-270.

Annotation: The authors monitored interactions between hikers and grizzly bears (*Ursus arctos*) in Montana's Glacier National Park during two consecutive summers. The level of trail use, presence of horses, and group size did not influence bear behavior during encounters. Although bear bells did not reduce the probability that hikers would encounter grizzlies, bears were less aggressive toward hikers with bear bells. The authors propose bears were able to anticipate encounters with hikers wearing bells and were thus less likely to charge hikers out of fear. Their findings suggest that habituation reduces aggressive bear behavior toward people in areas where bears are not conditioned to human foods.

Kasworm, W. F.; Manley, T. F. 1990. Road and trail influences on grizzly bears and black bears in northwest Montana. International Conference on Bear Research and Management. 8:79-84.

Annotation: See section IV.B.3. Page 59.

Linnell, John D. C.; Swenson, Jon E.; Andersen, Reidar; Barnes, Brian. 2000. How vulnerable are denning bears to disturbance? Wildlife Society Bulletin. 28(2):400-413.

Annotation: The authors conducted an extensive literature review to assess the potential for human disturbance of denning black (*Ursus americanus*), brown (*U. arctos*), and polar bears (*U. maritimus*). Reported weight losses for all species during winter were substantial (up to 40 percent in reproductive females), making them susceptible to increased energy expenditures due to den disturbance. Previous research showed that disturbed bears lost more weight than undisturbed bears and disturbed females with new-born cubs suffered greater cub mortalities than undisturbed females. Denning chronology, den type, and den location varied considerably among the three species and within the same species in different parts of its range. However, for black and brown bears, the denning period within a region appeared to be relatively predictable if autumn food abundance and snow conditions were monitored. Den sites were often located on steep, middle-elevation slopes. Management recommendations include restricting visitor activity in areas of high den concentrations and confining winter activity to regular routes (valley floors are preferable to slopes).

Mace, Richard D.; Waller, John S. 1996. Grizzly bear distribution and human conflicts in Jewel Basin Hiking Area, Swan Mountains, Montana. Wildlife Society Bulletin. 24(3):461-467.

Annotation: Telemetry locations were obtained from radiocollared grizzly bears (*Ursus arctos horribilis*) over the course of 8 years in a relatively small backcountry recreation area. No bears lived entirely within the recreation area, and their home ranges contained multiple-use lands with roads and hunting pressure. During the summer and fall, multivariate analyses indicated that bear locations were farther than expected from trails and lakes that had campsites. Bears also selected relatively open habitats compared to the forested habitat in which most of the trail system occurred. The authors suggest that low visitor-use levels, trail placement, an educated public, and the bears' negative conditioning toward human activities precluded bear-human conflicts in this area.

McLellan, Bruce N.; Shackleton, David M. 1989. Immediate reactions of grizzly bears to human activities. Wildlife Society Bulletin. 17(3):269-274.

Annotation: The authors monitored the behavioral response of grizzly bears (*Ursus arctos*) to several types of human stimuli (persons on foot, moving vehicles, heavy industrial equipment, fixed-wing aircraft, and helicopters) using both radiotelemetry and direct observations. The study occurred in the North Fork of the Flathead River drainage in Montana and British Columbia, where bears were exposed to many different types of human activity including hunting. Bears reacted most strongly (by running away) to people on foot than any other human stimulus, and this reaction was more pronounced in areas more than 500 m from a road. Bears also responded more strongly to ground-based activity (people on foot or moving vehicles) when bears were in the open rather than in cover. The authors suggest that bears in nearby Glacier National Park are less afraid of people due to habituation (see Jope and Shelby 1984).

Merrill, Evelyn H. 1978. Bear depredations at back-country campgrounds in Glacier National Park. Wildlife Society Bulletin. 6(3):123-126.

Annotation: See section IV.B.3. Pages 59.

Pitt, William C.; Jordan, Peter A. 1996. Influence of campsites on black bear habitat use and potential impact on caribou restoration. Restoration Ecology. 4(4):423-426.

Annotation: The authors used bait stations to survey black bears (*Ursus americanus*) in Minnesota's Boundary Waters Canoe Area Wilderness (BWCAW). Bears were found in areas near campsites more frequently than areas away from campsites, on both the mainland and on islands. This may have important implications for a proposed caribou (*Rangifer tarandus*) restoration effort in the BWCAW. Caribou in other locations typically choose islands as calving grounds, presumably to avoid predators. Thus, black bear use of islands with campsites in the BWCAW could lead to higher calf mortalities on those islands.

Purves, Helen D.; White, Clifford A.; Paquet, Paul C. 1992. Wolf and grizzly bear habitat use and displacement by human use in Banff, Yoho, and Kootenay National Parks: a preliminary analysis. Banff, Alberta: Canadian Parks Service. 49 p.

Annotation: See section IV.B.3. Page 59.

White, Don, Jr.; Kendall, Katherine C.; Picton, Harold D. 1999. Potential energetic effects of mountain climbers on foraging grizzly bears. Wildlife Society Bulletin. 27(1):146-151.

Annotation: The authors documented the effects of mountain climbers on foraging grizzly bears (*Ursus arctos horribilis*) in Glacier National Park, Montana. Bears were foraging on summer aggregations of adult army cutworm moths (*Euxoa auxiliaris*) in the alpine zone. When bears were disturbed by climbers, they spent less time foraging and more time moving compared to undisturbed bears. By estimating rates of moth consumption and analyzing the energy content of moths, the authors determined that feeding disruption cost bears approximately 12 kcal/minute in addition to the energy expended in moving about. Because moths are a seasonally important food source, the authors suggested that climbers be routed around moth sites used by bears.

2. Wolves

Creel, Scott; Fox, Jennifer E.; Hardy, Amanda; Sands, Jennifer; Garrott, Bob; Peterson, Rolf O. 2002. Snowmobile activity and glucocorticoid stress responses in wolves and elk. Conservation Biology. 16(3):809-814.

Annotation: See section III.B.1. Page 29.

Mech, L. David; Meier, Thomas J.; Burch, John W. 1991. Denali Park wolf studies: implications for Yellowstone. Transactions of the North American Wildlife and Natural Resources Conference. 56:86-90.

Annotation: The authors discussed the amount of protection from disturbance that is needed at wolf (*Canis lupus*) dens and rendezvous sites. Although wolves will sometimes relocate a den due to human disturbance, there has never been a record of wolf pups lost during such relocations. In Denali National Park, wolves at dens do not respond behaviorally to observers more than 0.8 km away, and one female raised a litter within 200 m of a road. The authors concluded that protection of wolf dens in National Parks would not require closing off large areas for extended periods of time.

Purves, Helen D.; White, Clifford A.; Paquet, Paul C. 1992. Wolf and grizzly bear habitat use and displacement by human use in Banff, Yoho, and Kootenay National Parks: a preliminary analysis. Banff, Alberta: Canadian Parks Service. 49 p.

Annotation: See section IV.B.3. Page 59.

Thiel, Richard P.; Merrill, Samuel; Mech, L. David. 1998. Tolerance by denning wolves, *Canis lupus*, to human disturbance. Canadian Field-Naturalist. 112:340-342.

Annotation: The authors provide recent anecdotal evidence that wolves (*Canis lupus*) can tolerate much greater human disturbance near den and rendezvous sites than previously thought. Wolf packs in Wisconsin, Minnesota, and Montana successfully reared pups in the immediate vicinity (less than 100 m in some cases) of heavy equipment use, helicopter logging, and military training. In one instance, after an active wolf den's entrance was buried by heavy equipment, the wolves moved 150 m into the forest and dug a new den. The following year, they re-excavated the old den and raised a new litter in it.

Thurber, J. M.; Peterson, Rolf O.; Drummer, T. D.; Thomasma, S. A. 1994. Gray wolf response to refuge boundaries and roads in Alaska. Wildlife Society Bulletin. 22(1):61-68.

Annotation: See section IV.B.3. Page 60.

Whittington, Jesse; St. Clair, Colleen C.; Mercer, George. 2005. Spatial responses of wolves to roads and trails in mountain valleys. Ecological Applications. 15(2):543-553.

Annotation: The authors aim to describe the impacts of human developments, such as roads, trails, and railways, on wolf behavior around Jasper, Alberta, Canada. They recorded the locations of wolf tracks from two wolf packs within 25 km of Jasper, and compared track locations within suitable wolf habitat around high- and low-use roads and trails. In the mountainous terrain of this study area, both wolf packs used low elevation, shallow slopes, and southwest aspects, probably because of lower snow depth and higher prey abundance in these areas. Both packs used low-use roads and trails more often than high-use roads and avoided areas with high road and/or trail density. Wolves traveled five times farther on low-use trails than high-use trails, but the low- and high-use road travel did not show the same magnitude of difference. The authors recommend that managers take into consideration the cumulative impact of roads and trails and manage the use of these to maintain high quality habitat for wolves.

3. Felines

Janis, Michael W.; Clark, Joseph D. 2002. Responses of Florida panthers to recreational deer and hog hunting. Journal of Wildlife Management. 66(3):839-848.

Annotation: Using radiotelemetry, the authors monitored Florida panther (*Puma concolor coryi*) movements before, during, and after the hunting season on protected lands in southwestern Florida. Hunting and its associated off-road vehicle use were allowed on part of the study area (treatment) and were not allowed on the rest of the study area (control). Panther responses to hunting were not detected for variables related to energy intake or expenditure (activity rates, movement rates, predation success). However, during the hunting season, panthers reduced their use of the most intensively hunted area, the Bear Island Unit, and increased their use of adjacent private land. This shift was thought to be in response to human activity, not prey movements.

McBride, Roy T.; Ruth, Toni K. 1988. Mountain lion behavior in response to visitor use in the Chisos Mountains of Big Bend National Park, Texas. Santa Fe, NM: U.S. Department of the Interior, National Park Service; Final Report CX-7130-0002. 35 p.

Annotation: Using radiotelemetry, the authors monitored mountain lion (*Felis concolor*) behavior and movements in response to human activity. Prior to this study, several incidents of mountain lion aggression toward humans had occurred within the Park. Mountain lions were most active at night, but there was considerable overlap between lion and human activity in the morning and evening. At night, mountain lions often used trails as travel corridors and passed close to campgrounds and designated backcountry campsites. Daytime bedsites were situated in proximity to trails on several occasions, and lion distance to the nearest trail was not correlated with the amount of trail use on that day. The authors suggested that three factors may contribute to aggressive lion behavior toward humans: (1) constant, but benign, exposure to humans resulting in habituation, (2) dispersal of food-stressed subadult lions, and (3) genetic predisposition of certain individuals.

Sunde, Peter; Stener, Snorre Ø.; Kvam, Tor. 1998. Tolerance to humans of resting lynxes *Lynx lynx* in a hunted population. Wildlife Biology. 4(3):177-183.

Annotation: The authors experimentally tested the daytime response of resting, radiocollared lynxes (*Lynx lynx*) to the approach of one or two persons on foot. The study was conducted in a rural, Norwegian landscape where lynxes are hunted. The median tolerance distance of lynxes to approaching humans was 50 m, and the median movement distance was 300 m. Lynxes tolerated a closer approach in mature, dense forests than in more open, younger forests. The authors suggested that lynxes can tolerate high human densities if sufficient mature forest habitat is present.

B. UNGULATES

A large number of studies exist of recreation impacts on deer, elk (*Cervus elaphus*), and bighorn sheep (*Ovis canadensis*). Most have measured immediate behavioral responses such as flight frequency, initial flight distance, and distance moved during flight. Interestingly, these species appear to be more sensitive to people on foot or skis than to motorized vehicles (Cassirer and others 2000; Freddy and others 1986; Hardy 2001; Papouchis and others 2001). The strongest reactions occur when a hiker is accompanied by a dog (MacArthur and others 1982, Miller and others 2001). Other studies have examined the effects of disturbance on habitat use (Etchberger and others 1989; Ferguson and Keith 1982; Hamilton and others 1982), energy consumption (Freddy and others 1986, Parker and others 1984), physiology (Hardy 2001; Krausman and others 1998; MacArthur and others 1982), and reproductive success (Phillips and Alldredge 2001). Studies on other ungulates are less common, but examples are provided for several species including bison (*Bison bison*), moose (*Alces alces*), and pronghorn antelope (*Antilocapra americana*).

1. Elk and Deer

Cassirer, E. Frances; Freddy, David J.; Ables, Ernest D. 1992. Elk responses to disturbance by cross-country skiers in Yellowstone National Park. Wildlife Society Bulletin. 20(4):375-381.

Annotation: Using an experimental approach, the authors measured the behavioral responses of wintering elk (*Cervus elaphus*) to persons on foot or cross-country skis in three different areas of the Park. Radiotelemetry and visual observations were used to determine the initial flight distance and distance moved by disturbed elk. Elk in more remote areas responded much more strongly than elk in the Mammoth Hot Springs area, which encountered people year-round. Thus, although elk can habituate to human activity, this may be a local phenomenon even in National Parks. In more remote areas, the median flight distance was 400 m and the median distance moved was 1,675 m. Disturbed elk temporarily moved up in elevation, to steeper slopes, and closer to forested areas. When moving away from skiers, elk were estimated to use about 5.5 percent of their average daily energy expenditure.

Creel, Scott; Fox, Jennifer E.; Hardy, Amanda; Sands, Jennifer; Garrott, Bob; Peterson, Rolf O. 2002. Snowmobile activity and glucocorticoid stress responses in wolves and elk. Conservation Biology. 16(3):809-814.

Annotation: Using a noninvasive technique, the authors tested for snowmobile effects on elk (*Cervus elaphus*) and wolves (*Canis lupus*) by assessing fecal glucocorticoid (GC) levels. Glucocorticoids moderate the long-term stress response in mammals, but chronically high levels can be detrimental to an animal's health (see Wingfield and Ramenofsky 1999). In Yellowstone National Park, daily elk fecal GC levels were correlated with the number of snowmobiles in the Park after controlling for the effects of snow depth and an animal's age. Wolf fecal GC levels during the winter were significantly higher in Voyageurs National Park than in Isle Royale National Park. Significant snowmobile use occurred in Voyageurs, whereas Isle Royale was closed to the general public during the winter. During the second winter of the study at Voyageurs, a decrease in fecal GC levels paralleled an identical decrease in snowmobile traffic. Although elk populations at Yellowstone and wolf populations at Voyageurs have been stable for 20 years or more, the authors believe that fecal GC levels provide a sensitive method of measuring stress before demographic responses become apparent.

Ferguson, Michael A. D.; Keith, Lloyd B. 1982. Influence of nordic skiing on distribution of moose and elk in Elk Island National Park, Alberta. Canadian Field-Naturalist. 96(1):69-78.

Annotation: Using aerial surveys and track and pellet counts, moose (*Alces alces*) and elk (*Cervus elaphus*) distributions were monitored over nine consecutive winters. After the first 3 years of the study, a cross-country-skiing trail network was established in the Park. Cross-country skiing appeared to displace moose, but not elk, from the area in which the trail system was established. Both species moved away from a trail, however, on days when skiers used the trail. The distance moved was not correlated with the number of skiers using the trail.

Freddy, David J.; Bronaugh, Whitcomb M.; Fowler, Martin C. 1986. Responses of mule deer to disturbance by persons afoot and snowmobiles. Wildlife Society Bulletin. 14(1):63-68.

Annotation: In this experimental study, marked mule deer (*Odocoileus hemionus*) were periodically exposed to persons afoot or on snowmobiles during two consecutive winters. The deer did not habituate to the experimental disturbances and were disturbed more by persons afoot. When approached on foot, they fled more frequently, at a greater distance from the source of disturbance, and for longer periods of time. When fleeing from persons on foot, deer were estimated to use 2 to 4 percent of their daily metabolic-energy requirements. Nonetheless, deer exposed to disturbance had similar mortality and fecundity rates as those in the local population.

Hardy, Amanda Ruth. 2001. Bison and elk responses to winter recreation in Yellowstone National Park. Bozeman, MT: Montana State University. 60 p. Thesis.

Annotation: Elk (*Cervus elaphus*) and bison (*Bison bison*) distribution, behavior, and fecal glucocorticoid (GC) levels were monitored over two winters to assess the potential impacts of winter recreation. Glucocorticoids are long-term stress hormones that may adversely affect wildlife if levels are chronically high. Recreation types included snowmobiling, driving wheeled snow vehicles, cross-country skiing, and snowshoeing. Behavioral responses were more frequent for both species when people were on foot and off-trail. Bison distribution and GC levels were not influenced by vehicle traffic, but elk were farther from roads and had higher GC levels on days of high traffic. Although the winter elk and bison population had been stable over the last 20 years despite increased winter visitation, the author recommended that Park managers use fecal GC sampling to monitor for physiological impacts before population declines become apparent.

Miller, Scott G.; Knight, Richard L.; Miller, Clinton K. 2001. Wildlife responses to pedestrians and dogs. Wildlife Society Bulletin. 29(1):124-132.

Annotation: In grasslands, the authors experimentally tested the behavioral response of mule deer (*Odocoileus hemionus*), vesper sparrows (*Pooecetes gramineus*), and western meadowlarks (*Sturnella neglecta*) to a hiker, a hiker with a leashed dog, and a dog alone. In forests, they tested the response of mule deer and American robins (*Turdus migratorius*) to a hiker and a hiker with a leashed dog. In both environments, all treatments were conducted on- and off-trail. For all species, initial flight distance and distance moved were greater for off-trail activities. Vesper sparrows and meadowlarks reacted more strongly to people than dogs, whereas mule deer reacted more strongly to dogs than people. Managers could reduce impacts in some areas by restricting hikers to trails, prohibiting dogs, or requiring dogs to be leashed.

Parker, K. L.; Robbins, C. T.; Hanley, T. A. 1984. Energy expenditures for locomotion by mule deer and elk. Journal of Wildlife Management. 48(2):474-488.

Annotation: The authors measured the energy expenditure of captive elk and mule deer (*Odocoileus hemionus*) as they moved through snow. Indirect calorimetry, which measures the oxygen content of respired air, was used to estimate energy use. Energy expenditures for movement through snow increased curvilinearly as a function of snow depth and density. Based on reported flight distances of elk and mule deer from winter recreationists in Yellowstone National Park, net energy expenditures per disturbance event were calculated. The authors concluded that disturbance from winter recreation could be an important factor in overwinter survival.

Phillips, Gregory E.; Alldredge, A. William. 2000. Reproductive success of elk following disturbance by humans during calving season. Journal of Wildlife Management. 64(2):521-530.

Annotation: In Colorado, the authors simulated hiking disturbance during the elk (*Cervus elaphus*) calving season to test for recreation impacts on elk fecundity. Pretreatment data was collected for 1 year at two neighboring locations. During the next 2 years, elk at the treatment location were repeatedly approached and displaced throughout a three-to-four-week period of peak calving, whereas elk at the control location were not approached. Throughout the study, calf:cow proportions remained stable at the control site but declined steadily at the treatment site, suggesting that repeated hiking disturbances can reduce reproductive success in elk. By modeling the demographic effect of decreased fecundity, the authors estimated that the experimental disturbances reduced annual population growth rates by 7 percent.

Taylor, Audrey R.; Knight, Richard L. 2003. Wildlife responses to recreation and associated visitor perceptions. Ecological Applications. 13(4):951-963.

Annotation: See section III.B.3. Page 31.

2. Bighorn Sheep

Etchberger, Richard C.; Krausman, Paul R.; Mazaika, Rosemary. 1989. Mountain sheep habitat characteristics in the Pusch Ridge Wilderness, Arizona. Journal of Wildlife Management. 53(4):902-907.

Annotation: Mountain sheep (*Ovis canadensis mexicana*) in the Pusch Ridge Wilderness (PRW) currently occupy about 18 percent of their historic range. The authors assessed differences in physiographic and vegetation variables between used and unused habitat. Sheep habitat was farther from human disturbance (hiking trails, roads, and housing developments) and was more open than unused habitat. Two factors appear to be limiting sheep distribution: (1) increased human disturbance in and around the PRW and (2) fire suppression, which has reduced the amount of open, high-visibility habitat.

Hamilton, Kathleen; Holl, Stephen A.; Douglas, Charles L. 1982. An evaluation of the effects of recreational activity on bighorn sheep in the San Gabriel Mountains, California. Desert Bighorn Council Transactions. 26:50-55.

Annotation: Bighorn sheep (*Ovis canadensis nelsoni*) use of mineral licks and habitat adjacent to hiking trails was compared between areas with different hiking intensities. The number and duration of bighorn visits were similar for a lick frequently passed by hikers and one rarely passed by hikers. In fact, at the more disturbed lick, the greatest proportion of sheep and hiker use both occurred during the midday hours. Bighorns did not avoid the lick but used it when hikers were not in the immediate vicinity. In addition, sheep use of habitat within 200 m of a heavily hiked trail did not differ from use near an infrequently traveled trail within the Cucamonga Wilderness.

King, Michael M.; Workman, Gar W. 1986. Response of desert bighorn sheep to human harassment: management implications. Transactions of the North American Wildlife and Natural Resources Conference. 51:74-85.

Annotation: In southeastern Utah, bighorn sheep behavioral responses to experimental approach by persons on foot or in vehicles were compared for two areas having different disturbance histories. Sheep in Red Canyon had been more intensively hunted and exposed to more vehicular traffic than sheep in White Canyon. Sheep in Red Canyon were more sensitive to disturbance, fleeing more often and farther and spending more time in alert behavior. This suggests that hunting may be incompatible with nonconsumptive activities and managers should consider disturbance history when managing human activities within bighorn habitat.

Krausman, Paul R.; Wallace, Mark C.; Hayes, Charles L.; DeYoung, Donald W. 1998. Effects of jet aircraft on mountain sheep. Journal of Wildlife Management. 62(4):1246-1254.

Annotation: The authors experimentally tested the response of mountain sheep (*Ovis canadensis nelsoni*) to low-level F-16 jet overflights. Six sheep were fitted with heart-rate monitors and contained in a 320-ha enclosure. Their heart rates and behavior were monitored before, during, and after a series of overflights occurring over the course of an entire year. Precise noise levels during overflights were measured throughout the enclosure. Heart rate increased during 21 of 149 overflights but returned to preflight levels within 120 seconds, and behavior and habitat use were not significantly altered by overflights. The authors concluded that jet overflights in National Parks, wilderness areas, and other public lands probably have little affect on sheep in these locations.

MacArthur, Robert A.; Geist, Valerius; Johnston, Ronald H. 1982. Cardiac and behavioral responses of mountain sheep to human disturbance. Journal of Wildlife Management. 46(2):351-358.

Annotation: The authors monitored the heart rates and behavioral responses of five free-ranging mountain sheep (*Ovis canadensis canadensis*) exposed to a variety of human activities including experimental approach by persons on foot. Cardiac and behavioral responses to approaching humans were greatest when the person was accompanied by a dog or approached sheep from over a ridge. Less than 10 percent of passing vehicles elicited a detectable heart-rate response, and no helicopters or fixed-wing aircraft farther than 400 m away elicited a response. The mean duration of heart-rate responses was similar to the mean duration of alert or withdrawal behaviors, but heart-rate responses were sometimes detected in the absence of behavioral cues.

Papouchis, Christopher M.; Singer, Francis J.; Sloan, William B. 2001. Responses of desert bighorn sheep to increased human recreation. Journal of Wildlife Management. 65(3):573-582.

Annotation: In Utah's Canyonlands National Park, the behavioral responses of desert bighorn sheep (*Ovis canadensis nelsoni*) to hikers, mountain bikers, and vehicles were observed. Hikers caused the most severe responses in terms of response frequency, distance fled, duration of response, and initial flight distance. The authors speculated that this occurred because hiker locations were less predictable and hikers approached sheep more frequently. Some sheep in a high-use area were habituated to human activity along the road, but most sheep avoided the road corridor. Males were more sensitive to human activity during the autumn rut, and females were more sensitive during the spring lambing period. The authors recommended that managers restrict hikers to trails during these critical periods.

Stockwell, Craig A.; Bateman, Gary C.; Berger, Joel. 1991. Conflicts in national parks: a case study of helicopters and bighorn sheep time budgets at the Grand Canyon. Biological Conservation. 56(3):317-328.

Annotation: To assess the impacts of helicopter overflights in the Park on desert bighorn sheep (*Ovis canadensis nelsoni*), the authors monitored sheep foraging activity during the winter and spring. During the winter, helicopter flights reduced sheep foraging efficiency by 43 percent. No effect was observed during the spring, perhaps because sheep had migrated to lower elevations. There appeared to be a disturbance threshold of 250 to 450 m. Potential impacts could be minimized by either restricting the number of flights or regulating the flight altitudes of helicopters.

3. Other Ungulates

Côté, Steeve D. 1996. Mountain goat responses to helicopter disturbance. Wildlife Society Bulletin. 24(4):681-685.

Annotation: In Alberta, Canada, mountain goat (*Oreamnos americanus*) behavioral responses to helicopter flights were observed during one summer. Goats were more adversely affected when helicopters approached within 500 m. Goats fled more than 100 m in 85 percent of these cases. Helicopter flights caused the disintegration of social groups on at least five occasions and resulted in one case of severe injury. Goats appeared to be more sensitive to helicopters than other open-terrain ungulates, and the author suggested the establishment of 2-km no-fly buffer zones around alpine areas and cliffs frequented by goats.

Duchesne, Mario; Côté, Steeve D.; Barrette, Cyrille. 2000. Responses of woodland caribou to winter ecotourism in the Charlevoix Biosphere Reserve, Canada. Biological Conservation. 96(3):311-317.

Annotation: The authors monitored woodland caribou (*Rangifer tarandus caribou*) behavior to assess the effects of winter ecotourism. In the presence of ecotourists, caribou spent more time being vigilant and standing and spent less time resting and foraging. As the number of visitors increased, caribou further reduced their foraging time. However, the caribou appeared to habituate to ecotourists as winter progressed, and visits were infrequent and short (11 total visits averaging less than 40 minutes). The authors believed that the caribou herd could tolerate continued small-scale ecotourism, particularly if group sizes were limited.

Fairbanks, W. Sue; Tullous, Randy. 2002. Distribution of pronghorn (*Antilocapra americana* Ord) on Antelope Island State Park, Utah, USA, before and after establishment of recreational trails. Natural Areas Journal. 22(4):277-282.

Annotation: The authors monitored the response of pronghorn antelope (*Antilocapra americana*) to the establishment of a new trail system used by hikers, horseback riders, and mountain bikers. Antelope distances to the nearest trail were recorded during the year before the trails were opened to the general public and the first 3 years afterwards. During all 3 years after the trails were opened, pronghorn groups were observed significantly farther from the trails. The smallest groups, which were composed of either males or females only, tended to be farther from trails than larger groups. This study demonstrated nonconsumptive recreation impacts on pronghorns for the first time.

Ferguson, Michael A. D.; Keith, Lloyd B. 1982. Influence of nordic skiing on distribution of moose and elk in Elk Island National Park, Alberta. Canadian Field-Naturalist. 96(1):69-78.

Annotation: See section III.B.1. Page 29.

Frid, Alejandro. 2003. Dall's sheep responses to overflights by helicopter and fixed-wing aircraft. Biological Conservation. 110(3):387-399.

Annotation: In Canada's Yukon Territory, Dall's sheep (*Ovis dalli dalli*) were experimentally exposed to overflights by a fixed-wing aircraft and helicopter. Sheep responded more strongly to helicopters than fixed-wing aircraft; all 25 groups fled when the minimum distance to the helicopter's flight trajectory was less than 0.5 km. Direct approaches by either type of aircraft were more likely to interrupt feeding or resting sheep. During indirect helicopter approaches, sheep far from rocky slopes were more likely to flee than sheep on rocky slopes. Previously resting sheep often had not resumed resting 20 minutes after exposure to overflights. Ungulates ruminate while resting, so overflights may disrupt energy assimilation by resting sheep.

Hardy, Amanda Ruth. 2001. Bison and elk responses to winter recreation in Yellowstone National Park. Bozeman, MT: Montana State University. 60 p. Thesis.

Annotation: See section III.B.1. Page 29.

Pitt, William C.; Jordan, Peter A. 1996. Influence of campsites on black bear habitat use and potential impact on caribou restoration. Restoration Ecology. 4(4):423-426.

Annotation: See section III.A.1. Page 27.

Taylor, Audrey R.; Knight, Richard L. 2003. Wildlife responses to recreation and associated visitor perceptions. Ecological Applications. 13(4):951-963.

Annotation: The authors studied recreation impacts on wildlife with respect to both biological and human dimensions. They measured the responses (alert distance, flight distance, and distance moved) of bison (*Bison bison*), mule deer (*Odocoileus hemionus*), and pronghorn antelope (*Antilocapra americana*) to solitary hikers and mountain bikers and found no significant difference between wildlife responses to the two different recreation types. All three species exhibited roughly a 70 percent probability of flushing when an on-trail recreationist was within 100m compared to a 96 percent probability of flushing for an off-trail recreator at the same distance. Secondly, the authors interviewed 640 backcountry trail users (hikers, bikers, horse riders) about their perceptions of the impact on their recreational activities on wildlife. They found half of those interviewed did not think that their recreational activities had any negative effects on wildlife. Additionally, recreationists felt that they could get much closer to wildlife without disturbing them than the researchers measured experimentally. Based on this study's results, the authors recommend limiting recreation to trails, establishing biologically based minimum approach distances to animals, and educating recreational users on the sensitivities of wildlife.

C. SMALL MAMMALS

Studies of recreation impacts on small mammals are uncommon and are limited mainly to rodents and bats. Due to their smaller home ranges, rodents can be affected by localized recreation impacts on vegetation and soils (Clevenger and Workman 1977; Foin and others 1977; Schmidly and Ditton 1979). Bat roosts in caves are subject to disturbance from spelunkers and cave explorers. Bats appear to be especially vulnerable to disturbance at winter roost sites (Humphrey 1978) and maternity colonies (Lacki 2000, Mann and others 2002). Cave gates are often used to protect important roost sites from human disturbance but can also affect bat behavior (Ludlow and Gore 2000, White and Seginak 1987).

1. Rodents

Clevenger, Gregory A.; Workman, Gar W. 1977. The effects of campgrounds on small mammals in Canyonlands and Arches National Parks, Utah. Transactions of the North American Wildlife and Natural Resources Conference. 42:473-484.

Annotation: Live trapping was conducted at one campground and a nearby control site in each Park to estimate the effects of campgrounds on small mammal populations. Overall, small mammals were more abundant in campgrounds than control sites. Specifically, Colorado chipmunks (*Eutamias quadrivittatus*), deer mice (*Peromyscus* spp.), and woodrats (*Neotoma* spp.) were significantly more abundant in at least one of the campgrounds. These species appear to be capable of exploiting human food sources in campgrounds. Campgrounds had a significant localized effect on small mammal populations, but the authors were unable to determine the extent of this effect.

Foin, T. C.; Garton, E. O.; Bowen, C. W.; Everingham, J. M.; Schultz, R. O.; Holton, B., Jr. 1977. Quantitative studies of visitor impacts on environments of Yosemite National Park, California, and their implications for Park management policy. Journal of Environmental Management. 5:1-22.

Annotation: The authors examined the impacts of trails and campgrounds to animal populations within meadow and forest environments in the Park. The amount of visitor use may have altered local rodent and bird communities. Deer mice (*Peromyscus maniculatus*) were more numerous in areas receiving more visitors, probably in response to the availability of additional food, but montane vole (*Microtus montanus*) abundance was not related to visitor densities. Several bird species were more abundant in campgrounds. Brewer's blackbird (*Euphagus cyanocephalus*) and the brown-headed cowbird (*Molothrus ater*) were found only in campgrounds. The Oregon junco (*Junco oreganus*), a ground-nesting species, was less abundant in campgrounds.

Mainini, Bruno; Neuhaus, Peter; Ingold, Paul. 1993. Behaviour of marmots *Marmota marmota* under the influence of different hiking activities. Biological Conservation. 64(2):161-164.

Annotation: In the Swiss Alps, the authors experimentally tested the behavioral responses of alpine marmots (*Marmota marmota*) to different types of hikers. The smallest response was to hikers staying on the trail, but the reaction increased when hikers were off-trail. Thus, the predictable location of hikers on trails appeared to be important. The strongest reactions, indicated by initial flight distance and the amount of time that marmots remained in their burrows, occurred when dogs were present.

Neuhaus, Peter; Mainini, Bruno. 1998. Reactions and adjustment of adult and young alpine marmots *Marmota marmota* to intense hiking activities. Wildlife Biology. 4(2):119-123.

Annotation: In the Swiss Alps, hikers directly approached alpine marmots (*Marmota marmota*) and recorded their behavioral responses. Marmots in heavily used areas showed less reaction to hikers than those in more remote areas. In adults, there was no change in responses over the course of the summer. Juveniles showed minor responses shortly after leaving the burrow, but in late summer, their responses increased greatly, particularly in more remote areas. Thus, the perception of danger appeared to be learned as the animal matured.

Schmidly, David J.; Ditton, Robert B. 1979. Assessing human impacts in two National Park areas of western Texas. In: Conference proceedings—recreational impact on wildlands. Tech. Rpt. R-6-001. U.S. Department of Agriculture, Forest Service, Pacific Northwest Research Station: 139-152.

Annotation: The authors measured rodent abundance and vegetation characteristics at riparian campsites in Big Bend National Park (BBNP) and Amistad Recreational

Area (ARA). At BBNP, tree density was lower at sites with higher visitor use, but there was no significant correlation between visitor use and the density of any rodent species or taxonomic family. At ARA, total rodent densities were higher at a campground than an unused control site. In addition, the campground's white-ankled mouse (*Peromyscus pectoralis*) population contained more juveniles and larger individuals in all age classes than the control site population. These differences may have been due to the presence of fewer predators and an enhanced food supply at the campground. Overgrazing by domestic livestock had a much greater impact on vegetation and rodent populations at BBNP and ARA than recreational use.

2. Bats

Humphrey, S. R. 1978. Status, winter habitat, and management of the endangered Indiana bat, *Myotis sodalis*. Florida Scientist. 41:65-76.

Annotation: Suspected reasons for the population decline of the Indiana bat (*Myotis sodalis*) were discussed. Because the majority of the total population hibernates in a handful of suitable caves, this species is extremely susceptible to human disturbance during the winter. Repeated disturbances by visitors and biologists can reduce a bat's fat reserves, resulting in high mortality during the spring. Steady population declines documented at some hibernation sites were likely due to high visitation rates or improperly designed bat gates, which disrupted cave temperatures. The author recommended that no more than one visit per year be permitted to each cave during the hibernation period. Cave access should be restricted using properly designed gates that allow the free circulation of air.

Lacki, Michael J. 2000. Effect of trail users at a maternity roost of Rafinesque's big-eared bats. Journal of Cave and Karst Studies. 62(3):163-168.

Annotation: Over a single breeding season, the author monitored a maternity colony of Rafinesque's big-eared bats (*Corynorhinus rafinesquii*) within a rock shelter adjacent to a hiking trail at Kentucky's Natural Bridge State Park. A 1-m wooden fence and a sign were installed by managers to discourage hikers from entering the shelter. The shelter was occupied by the colony from late April to mid-July, a period in which access was restricted by debris and washouts on the trail due to a severe storm the previous winter. However, after the trail was cleared of debris, the shelter was abandoned within 2 weeks. Some visitors using the trail were observed engaging in potentially disruptive behavior, and evidence of intrusions into the shelter was seen. This suggested that trail access may jeopardize the roost site.

Ludlow, Mark E.; Gore, Jeffery A. 2000. Effects of a cave gate on emergence patterns of colonial bats. Wildlife Society Bulletin. 28(1):191-196.

Annotation: The authors documented changes in emergence patterns of southeastern myotis (*Myotis austroriparius*) and gray bats (*M. grisescens*) after the removal of a steel-bar gate

from a Florida cave. Emerging bats were counted monthly at an open entrance and the gated entrance for 1 year before and after removal of the gate. Although the total number of bats emerging from both entrances did not change after gate removal, the number of bats using the gated entrance increased significantly. Before gate removal, only 7.8 percent of the bats used the gated entrance, after gate removal, 47.9 percent of the bats emerged from this entrance. Bats may have avoided the gated entrance because snakes sometimes used the gate as a hunting perch. Perimeter fencing is recommended as an alternative to steel-bar gates at caves where trespassing and vandalism are not chronic problems.

Mann, Sherry L.; Steidl, Robert J.; Dalton, Virginia M. 2002. Effects of cave tours on breeding *Myotis velifer*. Journal of Wildlife Management. 66(3):618-624.

Annotation: In Arizona, the authors assessed the behavioral responses of a maternity colony of cave myotis bats (*Myotis velifer*) to experimental cave tours. Maternity colonies are vulnerable to human disturbance because suitable colony sites may be limited and most bats raise only one young per year. Three factors were manipulated: light intensity and color, size of tour groups, and whether tour groups talked or not. Light intensity affected bat behavior the most. All measures of bat activity were highest with high-intensity white light and lowest with no light. Bat activity level also increased when tour groups talked, the maternity season progressed, and bats roosted closer to the tour route. The authors recommended that no tours should not be allowed in roosting areas during the maternity period. Cave tours can also be designed to minimize their effects on roosting bats.

Speakman, J. R.; Webb, P. I.; Racey, P. A. 1991. Effects of disturbance on the energy expenditure of hibernating bats. Journal of Applied Ecology. 28:1087-1104.

Annotation: Twenty-five individual bats of six European species were placed within respirometry chambers and exposed to both nontactile stimuli (light, sound, temperature increase) and tactile stimuli. Less than 5 percent of the nontactile exposures caused a significant increase in energy expenditure, whereas all of the tactile exposures caused a significant increase. In addition, the amount of energy expended during a response was much greater for tactile stimuli (2038 J) than nontactile stimuli (49 J). Degree of response to a tactile stimulation increased significantly with increasing body mass. When extrapolated over an entire hibernation period, nontactile disturbances appeared to have a negligible effect on fat depletion and reduction in the potential duration of hibernation. However, the authors noted that bat responses may have been influenced by being inside a respirometry chamber and having been torpid for a relatively short period of time before the experiment.

White, Donald H.; Seginak, John T. 1987. Cave gate designs for use in protecting endangered bats. Wildlife Society Bulletin. 15(3):445-449.

Annotation: The authors tested the preferences of two endangered bat species, gray myotis (*Myotis grisescens*) and

Townsend's big-eared (*Plecotus townsendii*), for three different designs of bat gate. The gate designs consisted of horizontally placed angle irons, a grid of round steel bars, and a funnel. Both species avoided the funnel design. Gray myotis showed no preference for either the angle-iron or steel-bar design, but big-eared bats preferred the steel-bar design. However, the angle-iron gate was more resistant to human trespassers. On five occasions, the steel-bar gates were breached by people who pried the bars apart or cut them with a hacksaw. Managers may need to consider the added security provided by angle-iron gates when selecting a gate design.

D. RAPTORS

Extensive research has been conducted on recreation impacts to raptors, particularly for the bald eagle (*Haliaeetus leucocephalus*). Behavioral responses, such as flight frequency and initial flight distance, are typically measured and a variety of factors can influence flush responses. Of special note, raptors appear to be more sensitive to people on foot than to vehicles, boats, or aircraft (Grubb and others 1992; Grubb and King 1991; Holmes and others 1993; Stalmaster and Kaiser 1998). Other raptor studies examine the effects of disturbance on habitat use (Fletcher and others 1999; McGarigal and others 1991; Stalmaster and Kaiser 1998), parental care behavior (Fernández and Azkona 1993, Steidl and Anthony 2000), and reproductive success (Fernández and Azkona 1993, Fraser and others 1985).

1. Bald eagle

Anthony, Robert G.; Steidl, Robert J.; McGarigal, Kevin. 1995. Recreation and bald eagles in the Pacific Northwest. In: Knight, Richard L.; Gutzwiller, Kevin J., eds. Wildlife and recreationists: coexistence through management and research. Washington, DC: Island Press: 223-241.

Annotation: The authors discuss recreation impacts and options for managing recreation use near bald eagles (*Haliaeetus leucocephalus*). Although the chapter title suggests a focus on the Pacific Northwest, studies from throughout the United States are cited. Most research has focused on the short-term effects of recreation on bald eagle behavior. Active displacement occurs along narrow river corridors when eagles flush upon close approach by recreationists. Passive displacement occurs on large bodies of water when eagles avoid foraging in areas receiving high human use. Long-term effects on eagle fitness are possible but difficult to document. The authors discuss the following management options: spatial and temporal restrictions on recreational activities, habitat management, and visitor education.

Fraser, James D.; Frenzel, L. D.; Mathisen, John E. 1985. The impact of human activities on breeding bald eagles in north-central Minnesota. Journal of Wildlife Management. 49(3):585-592.

Annotation: The authors studied the effects of various human activities on bald eagle (*Haliaeetus leucocephalus*) nesting success over the course of 3 years. No differences were detected between successful and unsuccessful nests in terms of human activity within 500 m of the nest. Human activities included road traffic, pedestrians, and recreation areas. In addition, responses to hikers were determined by deliberately approaching four eagle nests on foot at least five times each. Average initial flight distance was nearly 500 m and was correlated with the number of previous experimental disturbances, date, and time of day. Habituation to repeated intrusions did not occur, as initial flight distance increased during later approaches. In contrast, incubating or brooding eagles never flushed from the nest in response to fixed-wing aircraft passing within 20 to 200 m during weekly nest surveys.

Grubb, Teryl G.; Bowerman, WilliamW.; Giesy, John P.; Dawson, Gary A. 1992. Responses of breeding bald eagles, *Haliaeetus leucocephalis*, to human activities in northcentral Michigan. Canadian Field-Naturalist. 106:443-453.

Annotation: Breeding bald eagle (*Haliaeetus leucocephalus*) responses to all human activity near nest sites were recorded. Aircraft flights and boating were the most common human activities occurring near nest sites, but vehicles and pedestrians induced the highest response frequencies. Seventy-five percent of all alert and flight responses occurred when activity was within 500 m and 200 m, respectively. Adults flushed more easily when perched away from the nest and flushed more frequently than nestlings. Similar to study conducted in Arizona (Grubb and King 1991), disturbance distance was the most important predictor of eagle responses, followed by disturbance duration, number of persons or craft per event, and visibility. These two studies support the traditional use of distance-based buffer zones as a management technique, although local verification of response frequencies and distances should be performed.

Grubb, Teryl G.; King, Rudy M. 1991. Assessing human disturbance of breeding bald eagles with classification tree models. Journal of Wildlife Management. 55(3):500-511.

Annotation: In central Arizona, the authors observed breeding bald eagle (*Haliaeetus leucocephalus*) responses to human activity occurring near nest sites. Human activities included pedestrians, boats, vehicles, and aircraft. Pedestrians (hikers, anglers, hunters) induced the highest response frequency and the longest response duration. Bald eagles were flushed from perches more frequently than nests and were most easily disturbed when foraging. According to classification tree models, the most important predictor of eagle response was disturbance distance, followed by disturbance duration, visibility, and number of persons or craft per event (see Grubb and others 1992).

McGarigal, Kevin; Anthony, Robert G.; Isaacs, Frank B. 1991. Interactions of humans and bald eagles on the Columbia River estuary. Wildlife Monographs. 115:1-47.

Annotation: The authors used an experimental approach to determine the effects of boating on breeding bald eagles (*Haliaeetus leucocephalus*). On the study area, the predominant human-eagle interaction involved passive displacement of eagles from foraging sites by boats. At three different stages of the nesting period, a breeding eagle pair was monitored during a 3-day control period to identify normal foraging behavior. This was followed by a 3-day disturbance period, in which a stationary boat with an observer was placed in the center of a pair's high-use foraging area. Eagles typically avoided the area within 400 m of the stationary boat, and responses were consistent among nesting stages. The authors developed a conceptual, dual-disturbance-threshold model, which can be applied to both moving and stationary human activities. Spatial and temporal restrictions on human activities and active management of eagle habitat (for example, providing artificial foraging perches in areas where perches are limited) were recommended.

Montopoli, George J.; Anderson, Donald A. 1991. A logistic model for the cumulative effects of human intervention on bald eagle habitat. Journal of Wildlife Management. 55(2):290-293.

Annotation: See section IV.B.3. Page 59.

Skagen, Susan K.; Knight, Richard L.; Orians, Gordon H. 1991. Human disturbance of an avian scavenging guild. Ecological Applications. 1(2):215-225.

Annotation: See section II.C.3. Page 21.

Stalmaster, Mark V.; Kaiser, James L. 1998. Effects of recreational activity on wintering bald eagles. Wildlife Monographs. 137:1-46.

Annotation: The authors used observational and experimental techniques to assess the effects of recreation on wintering bald eagles (*Haliaeetus leucocephalus*) in Washington's Skagit River Bald Eagle Natural Area. As recreational activity increased along the river, eagles foraged less frequently and were displaced to perches away from the river. Eagles were most sensitive to recreation when feeding on the ground and during the morning, a time that undisturbed eagles foraged intensively. Individual eagles responded most strongly to foot traffic. However, boat traffic had a greater effect on the overall population because of its more frequent, widespread occurrence. When experimentally approached by a boat, subadults flushed more readily than adults, and eagles next to narrow river channels flushed more often than those next to wide channels. When surveyed, river recreationists substantially underestimated their impact on eagles in terms of flush distance and distance flown, and only 26 percent believed that recreational use was having an adverse effect on eagles. The authors recommended prohibiting recreation within 400 m of eagles during the first 5 hours of daylight, restricting foot traffic

and motorboats, and providing public education to increase support for management actions.

Steidl, Robert J.; Anthony, Robert G. 1996. Responses of bald eagles to human activity during the summer in interior Alaska. Ecological Applications. 6(2):482-491.

Annotation: During four consecutive summers, bald eagles (*Haliaeetus leucocephalus*) along a relatively remote stretch of Alaska's Gulkana River were approached by a nonmotorized boat to determine their response rates and initial flight distances. Breeding adults flushed less frequently and tolerated closer approaches than nonbreeding adults. The response rate of nonbreeding adults decreased, however, as perch height and distance from the river increased. In addition, eagles along the least frequently used stretch of the river had the greatest response rates and initial flight distances. In contrast, the initial flight distances for this study were well below those reported in other studies where human activity was greater. The authors did not hypothesize any reasons for this apparent difference across spatial scales in the effects of human use level on sensitivity to disturbance. Along narrow wilderness rivers such as the Gulkana, the authors recommended the use of temporal, rather than spatial, restrictions on recreational use.

Steidl, Robert J.; Anthony, Robert G. 2000. Experimental effects of human activity on breeding bald eagles. Ecological Applications. 10(1):258-268.

Annotation: Along Alaska's Gulkana River, the authors experimentally determined the effects of nearby campsites on bald eagle (*Haliaeetus leucocephalus*) nesting behavior. The treatment consisted of researchers camping for 24 hours at a distance of 100 m from the nest, and the control consisted of camping at a distance of 500 m from the nest. When campers were close to nests, adult eagles significantly decreased the amount of time spent preening, maintaining the nest, and feeding themselves and the nestlings, and increased the time spent brooding the nestlings. Over the course of the 24-hour period, eagle responses to nearby campers diminished, suggesting that the eagles began to habituate. Nonetheless, during the last 4 hours of treatment, adults still vocalized twice as frequently as controls, indicating continued agitation. By altering eagle nesting behavior, frequent human activities near nests could adversely affect nestling survival.

2. Other Raptors

Fernández, Carmelo; Azkona, Paz. 1993. Human disturbance affects parental care of marsh harriers and nutritional status of nestlings. Journal of Wildlife Management. 57(3):602-608.

Annotation: At a protected reserve in Spain, the authors studied the effects of human activities (nearby fishermen, hikers, dogs, vehicles) on nesting marsh harriers (*Circus aeruginosus*). During periods of disturbance, the parents delivered fewer food items to the nest and spent less time at the nest, especially during the incubation period. In addition, disturbed birds spent more time giving alarm calls, chasing other birds, and flying. Although the reproductive output at nests experiencing disturbance was similar to that of nearby undisturbed nests, blood urea levels indicated that nestlings of disturbed birds were in poorer physical condition. Thus, human disturbance may not affect immediate reproductive success but may reduce lifetime reproductive success by affecting the long-term survival of nestlings or adults.

Fletcher, Robert J., Jr.; McKinney, Shawn T.; Bock, Carl E. 1999. Effects of recreational trails on wintering diurnal raptors along riparian corridors in a Colorado grassland. Journal of Raptor Research. 33(3):233-239.

Annotation: Wintering raptor abundances along a riparian corridor were estimated at three sites with recreational trails and three sites without trails. Seven species of raptors were sighted during the study: red-tailed hawk (*Buteo jamaicensis*), bald eagle (*Haliaeetus leucocephalus*), rough-legged hawk (*B. lagopus*), ferruginous hawk (*B. regalis*), northern harrier (*Circus cyaneus*), golden eagle (*Aquila chrysaetos*), and prairie falcon (*Falco mexicanus*). Although there were no significant differences in habitat structure or perch availability between the sites, species richness and abundance were greater at sites without trails. At sites without trails, raptors also perched closer to the riparian corridor. Whereas red-tailed hawk abundance was similar at sites with and without trails, other raptors were less abundant at sites with trails. The authors suggest that red-tailed hawks have better adapted to human development and activity.

Holmes, Tamara L.; Knight, Richard L.; Stegall, Libby; Craig, Gerald R. 1993. Responses of wintering grassland raptors to human disturbance. Wildlife Society Bulletin. 21(4):461-468.

Annotation: In Colorado, the authors experimentally tested the responses of six diurnal raptor species to approach by humans on foot and in vehicles. The six species were rough-legged hawk (*Buteo lagopus*), ferruginous hawk (*B. regalis*), prairie falcon (*Falco mexicanus*), American kestrel (*F. sparverius*), merlin (*F. columbarius*), and golden eagle (*Aquila chrysaetos*). Overall, 97 percent of the birds flushed when approached on foot compared to 38 percent when approached by a car traveling at 70 km per hour. All species, except for prairie falcons, flushed more frequently in response to persons on foot. Furthermore, larger species flushed at a greater distance when approached on foot. Management plans, especially those utilizing spatial buffer zones, should be tailored to individual species and type of disturbance.

Knight, Richard L.; Skagen, Susan Knight. 1988. Effects of recreational disturbance on birds of prey: a review. In: Glinski, Richard L.; Pendleton, Beth Giron; Moss, Mary Beth; LeFranc, Maurice N., Jr.; Millsap, Brian A.; Hoffman, Stephen W., eds. Proceedings of the Southwest raptor management symposium and workshop. Scientific and Technical Series No. 11. Washington, DC: National Wildlife Federation, Institute for Wildlife Research: 355-359.

Annotation: The authors review the literature regarding recreational effects on raptors. Recreational disturbance has been shown to impact raptors by: (1) altering their distribution, (2) disrupting parental care of nestlings, (3) causing abandonment of breeding territories, (4) reducing reproductive success, and (5) affecting their foraging behavior. The use of spatial and temporal restrictions on recreation is advocated, rather than completely denying human access to areas containing raptors. To improve our current knowledge of recreational effects on raptors, the authors suggest treating management actions in an experimental context.

Swarthout, Elliott C. H.; Steidl, Robert J. 2003. Experimental effects of hiking on breeding Mexican spotted owls. Conservation Biology. 17(1):307-315.

Annotation: In Utah's Canyonlands and Capitol Reef National Parks, the authors experimentally assessed the effects of hiking on nesting Mexican spotted owls (*Strix occidentalis lucida*). Spotted owl activity was monitored at nest sites receiving both control and hiking treatments. During hiking treatments, a person hiked past the nest once every 15 minutes. In general, owl behavior did not change substantially when exposed to hiking, although both sexes increased their use of contact vocalizations. Given the current levels of hiking in most of the remote canyons occupied by owls, current restrictions are not needed. However, monitoring of owls and hiking intensity was recommended for canyons visited by 50 or more hikers per day.

Wildman, Ann Marie. 1992. The effect of human activity on great gray owl hunting behavior in Yosemite National Park, California. Tech. Rep. NPS/WRUC/NRTR-92/49. Davis, CA: U.S. Department of the Interior, National Park Service, Western Region, and Cooperative National Park Studies Unit, University of California-Davis. 87 p. *(Note: This document can be ordered by calling 209-372-0280.)*

Annotation: Four great gray owls (*Strix nebulosa*) that foraged at meadows visited by hikers and birdwatchers were monitored to assess visitor impacts on the owls. Owls were occasionally flushed by visitors. Initial flight distance increased with the distance at which an owl detected people, with larger group sizes, and when owls were hunting rather than resting. However, the author concluded that owl foraging behavior and reproductive success were mainly influenced by weather and prey availability, not by interactions with visitors.

E. WATERBIRDS

Management strategies for recreation near waterbirds largely depend on whether the birds are colonial or solitary breeders. Colonial breeders are more easily protected because nesting occurs at fixed, easily identified locations (Burger 1995). Studies of colonial nesters have focused on nest occupancy (Anderson 1988, Skagen and others 2001), nesting success (Bolduc and Guillemette 2003, Anderson and Keith 1980), and initial flight distances (Erwin 1989; Rodgers and Smith 1995, 1997). Carney and Sydeman

(1999) conducted a literature review for colonial nesters, but see Nisbet (2000) for a critique of this review and of disturbance studies in general. Studies of solitary breeders such as shorebirds and waterfowl have focused on nesting success (Flemming and others 1988; Götmark and others 1989; Keller 1989; Titus and VanDruff 1981), initial flight distances (Lafferty 2000, Rodgers and Smith 1997), energetic costs (Morton 1996, Bélanger and Bédard 1990; Morton and others 1989), and food consumption (Gill and others 2001b). Madsen and Fox (1995) provide a review of the effects of hunting disturbance on waterfowl.

1. Colonial Nesters

Anderson, Daniel W. 1988. Dose-response relationship between human disturbance and brown pelican breeding success. Wildlife Society Bulletin. 16(3):339-345.

Annotation: On an isolated island in Mexico's Gulf of California, the author studied the effect of human disturbance on a California brown pelican (*Pelecanus occidentalis californicus*) breeding colony. After a fishing camp was established on the island, breeding brown pelicans gradually abandoned their nests over the next several years, eventually deserting the island altogether. During this time, nest occupancy was strongly correlated with distance to the nearest disturbance (trail or camp). Pelicans began to abandon nests when disturbance occurred within 600 m.

Anderson, Daniel W.; Keith, James O. 1980. The human influence on seabird nesting success: conservation implications. Biological Conservation. 18:65-80.

Annotation: In this often-cited paper, the authors observed a decrease in reproductive success in portions of brown pelican (*Pelecanus occidentalis californicus*) and Heermann's gull (*Larus heermanni*) colonies experiencing human disturbance. Conducted on islands near Baja California, Mexico, the study documented disturbances involving recreationists, educational groups, local fishermen, and scientists. Disturbance impacted brown pelican nest success by: (1) exposing eggs and nestlings to gull and raven predation, hyperthermia, and hypothermia and (2) causing nest abandonment during the early stages of nesting. Disturbance impacted Heermann's gull nest success by exposing eggs and nestlings to intra-specific predation. More stringent protective measures were called for, including the total exclusion of humans when necessary.

Bolduc, François; Guillemette, Magella. 2003. Human disturbance and nesting success of Common Eiders: interaction between visitors and gulls. Biological Conservation. 110:77-83.

Annotation: The authors address the effects of frequency and timing of human disturbance on bird nesting success. Their study focused on several, remote, nesting colonies of Common Eiders (*Somateria mollissima*) in a national park reserve in Canada that would be potentially visited by scientists, down collectors, and eco-tourists. Mimicking the most invasive visit that might occur, by walking up to

nests and flushing the females as down collectors do, the authors compared impacts of high versus low frequency of human visitation occurring early versus late in the nesting season. They found that the first visit to a colony, regardless of when that first visit occurred, accounted for 40 to 70 percent of nest failures. Subsequent visits were correlated with minimal additional failures, and no additional failures in frequently visited colonies. Regarding the timing of disturbance, flushing distance of females decreased as incubation stage increased. The increased nest success at colonies that were visited later was attributed to the greater likelihood of females defending their nests at this stage. The authors were unable to compare their results to a control (unvisited colony). However, because of the large impact of first visits they observed, regardless of timing in the nesting cycle, they recommend that managers do not allow any close visitation of Common Eider nests.

Burger, Joanna. 1995. Beach recreation and nesting birds. In: Knight, Richard L.; Gutzwiller, Kevin J., eds. Wildlife and recreationists: coexistence through management and research. Washington, DC: Island Press: 281-295.

Annotation: See section III.E.2. Page 39.

Burger, J.; Gochfeld, M. 1998. Effects of ecotourists on bird behaviour at Loxahatchee National Wildlife Refuge, Florida. Environmental Conservation. 25(1):13-21.

Annotation: To address a paucity of information about human disturbance to foraging birds, the authors observed bird species in a part of the Florida everglades that was heavily visited by tourists. The five species studied (common gallinule (*Gallinula chloropus*), sora rail (*Porzana carolina*), glossy ibis (*Plegadis falcinellus*), little blue heron (*Egretta caerulea*), and Lousiana heron (*Egretta tricolor*)) were chosen because they represent a range of sensitivity to human disturbance. The authors watched foraging birds as people approached on nearby trails and recorded bird behaviors at three times: before people approached, when the people were closest to the birds, and when they were >10 m away again. They measured foraging and vigilant behaviors, and compared them with tourist group metrics. They found when people approached, the birds moved away, devoted less time to foraging, made fewer strikes at food, and were more vigilant. The number of people in the group and loudness of tourist groups correlated with increased behavioral responses. Following disturbances, birds spent less time foraging and more time being vigilant. Although there were differences in initial responses and recovery time among bird species, all birds altered their behaviors upon tourists' approaches, regardless of the predictability of tourist presence on trails.

Carney, Karen M.; Sydeman, William J. 1999. A review of human disturbance effects on nesting colonial waterbirds. Waterbirds. 22(1):68-79.

Annotation: The authors reviewed 64 published investigations concerning human disturbance effects on nesting colonial waterbirds. Research findings were summarized for each of five taxonomic groups, by disturbance type (scientific research, visitor, aircraft/watercraft) and the measured response variable (for example, reproductive success). Previous research has largely focused on researcher disturbance, which is often intense—entering colonies, handling nest contents, and capturing adults. In contrast, fewer studies have examined the impacts of ecotourists and recreationists, whose peak use of natural areas coincide with the breeding season of colonial waterbirds. Based on the literature, specific recommendations are provided to minimize both researcher and visitor disturbance of each taxonomic group. For a critique of this review, see Nisbet (2000).

Erwin, R. Michael. 1989. Responses to human intruders by birds nesting in colonies: experimental results and management guidelines. Colonial Waterbirds. 12(1):104-108.

Annotation: Nesting colonies of wading birds and seabirds in Virginia and North Carolina were approached by persons on foot to assess their sensitivity to human disturbance. Mixed colonies of common terns (*Sterna hirundo*) and black skimmers (*Rynchops niger*) responded at the greatest distances with "dread" flights (individuals from the entire colony flew in a circle and landed again). Mixed colonies of wading birds were more reluctant to flush. In general, initial flight distance did not appear to be related to colony size or nesting stage. To protect colonies from disturbance, the author recommended a 100-m buffer zone for wading birds and some tern species and a 200-m buffer zone for common terns and black skimmers.

Kaiser, Mark S.; Fritzell, Erik K. 1984. Effects of river recreationists on green-backed heron behavior. Journal of Wildlife Management. 48(2):561-567.

Annotation: Along four stretches of Missouri's Ozark National Scenic Riverway, the authors examined the effects of recreational use on green-backed heron (*Butorides striatus*) habitat use. On three of the river stretches, heron abundance on the main river channel decreased strongly as the number of recreationist groups increased. However, heron abundance on backwater areas adjacent to the river was not correlated with recreational use. Thus, herons displaced from the main river channel did not appear to relocate to adjacent backwater areas. Recreational use was highest on weekends, and most of the disrupted heron foraging bouts on weekends were due to human disturbance.

Nisbet, Ian C. T. 2000. **Disturbance, habituation, and management of waterbird colonies.** Waterbirds. 23(2):312-332.

Annotation: The author critiques previous studies that have reported human disturbance effects on breeding colonial waterbirds, including the review conducted by Carney and Sydeman (1999). He emphasizes that the effects of "disturbance" are not always adverse and that many studies have failed to adequately control for other influential factors such as weather, predation, and food availability. Precise definitions for "disturbance," "habituation," and "tolerance" and a classification scheme for types of disturbance and effects are proposed. In addition, an extensive review of the

literature on human disturbance in tern colonies is presented. The author recommends that carefully managed visits to colonies should be maximized, rather than minimized, to deliberately promote habituation.

Rodgers, James A., Jr.; Smith, Henry T. 1995. Setback distances to protect nesting bird colonies from human disturbance in Florida. Conservation Biology. 9(1):89-99.

Annotation: Throughout northern and central Florida, the authors experimentally approached nesting colonies of 15 waterbird species to determine initial flight distances for each species. Colonies were approached by persons on foot, in a canoe, and in a motorboat. Most species flushed at greater distances when approached by walkers compared to approach by boats. A formula was developed for determining a conservative set-back distance, or buffer zone, based on initial flight distances (see Rodgers and Smith 1997). When establishing buffer zones around mixed-species colonies, the most sensitive species should be used to set the distance. For the sites used in this study, a buffer zone of 100 m for wading bird colonies and 180 m for mixed tern/skimmer colonies should provide adequate protection from pedestrian or boat traffic.

Rodgers, James A., Jr.; Smith, Henry T. 1997. Buffer zone distances to protect foraging and loafing waterbirds from human disturbance in Florida. Wildlife Society Bulletin. 25(1):139-145.

Annotation: Throughout northern and central Florida, the authors experimentally approached nonbreeding waterbirds from 16 species to determine initial flight distances for each species. Flocks were approached by persons on foot, on an all-terrain vehicle, in a canoe, and in a motorboat. Most within-species flight distances were similar for each disturbance type, and shorebirds often had the lowest initial flight distances. Among the colonial-nesting species, flight distances for nonbreeding birds were frequently greater than those previously recorded for nesting birds. A formula was used to determine a conservative set-back distance, or buffer zone, around foraging and resting birds based on initial flight distances (see Rodgers and Smith 1995). A 100-m buffer zone should minimize disturbance to most species of Florida waterbirds included in this study.

Skagen, Susan K.; Melcher, Cynthia P.; Muths, Erin. 2001. The interplay of habitat change, human disturbance and species interactions in a waterbird colony. American Midland Naturalist. 145(1):18-28.

Annotation: At Colorado's Chatfield State Recreation Area, a mixed breeding colony of great blue herons (*Ardea herodias*) and double-crested cormorants (*Phalacrocorax auritus*) was monitored for 2 years prior to and 2 years after the construction of a wildlife viewing area. During this time, the number of active heron nests and heron nest success declined. The authors suggest that this decline resulted from a combination of factors: habitat change (14 of 31 original nest trees lost to windfall), acquisition of heron nests by cormorants, and greater sensitivity of herons to disturbance (as evidenced by a shift in heron nest locations away from the viewing area during the study). Cormorants did not appear to be affected by the viewing area.

2. Solitary Nesters

Bélanger, Luc; Bédard, Jean. 1990. Energetic cost of man-induced disturbance to staging snow geese. Journal of Wildlife Management. 54(1):36-41.

Annotation: The authors estimated the effect of human disturbance on the energy balance of fall-staging greater snow geese (*Chen caerulescens atlantica*) in Québec, Canada. The main sources of disturbance on the study area were hunting and aircraft overflights. Two responses to disturbance were evaluated: (1) birds flew away but promptly returned and resumed feeding and (2) birds flew away and stopped feeding altogether. Both types of response resulted in a projected energy deficit. Furthermore, no increase in daytime feeding rate was observed on days with higher levels of disturbance. Thus, birds would need to increase their nighttime feeding rates to compensate for disturbance-induced energy losses.

Burger, Joanna. 1995. Beach recreation and nesting birds. In: Knight, Richard L.; Gutzwiller, Kevin J., eds. Wildlife and recreationists: coexistence through management and research. Washington, DC: Island Press: 281-295.

Annotation: In many regions, beaches are important areas for both human recreationists and breeding birds. This chapter reviews the effects of beach recreation on nesting shorebirds, terns, and skimmers. Although the author emphasizes studies conducted in New Jersey, the relationships and management recommendations are more broadly applicable. Observed effects include the abandonment of least tern breeding colonies and the disruption of piping plover foraging. Management options for reducing the impacts of recreational use on nesting birds depend largely on whether a species is a colonial or a solitary nester. Solitary-nesting birds are more difficult to protect because they occur over much larger areas of beach. Potential management options for each nesting strategy are discussed including visitor education, active protection (fences, signs, wardens, predator control), and beach closures. In addition, the creation of sandy shoals or islands away from areas of human activity has successfully attracted colonial nesters such as least terns and black skimmers.

Burger, J., Gochfeld, M. 1998. Effects of ecotourists on bird behaviour at Loxahatchee National Wildlife Refuge, Florida. Environmental Conservation. 25(1):13-21.

Annotation: See section III.E.1. Page 37.

Flemming, Stephen P.; Chiasson Roland D.; Smith, Peter C.; Austin-Smith, Peter J.; Bancroft, Robert P. 1988. Piping plover status in Nova Scotia related to its reproductive and behavioral responses to human disturbance. Journal of Field Ornithology. 59(4):321-330.

Annotation: The authors suggested that human disturbance may be partly responsible for the range-wide population decline of the threatened piping plover (*Charadrius melodus*). During a period of substantial decline in Nova Scotia, pedestrian and vehicle traffic was monitored on nesting beaches. Nests experiencing higher disturbance levels produced significantly fewer young surviving to 17 days of age. During disturbance events, chicks decreased their time spent feeding and brooding and increased their time spent being vigilant. When feeding did occur, it was at a reduced rate. Thus, disturbance may have impacted chick energy reserves, which resulted in reduced chick survival rates.

Gill, Jennifer A.; Norris, Ken; Sutherland, William J. 2001b. The effects of disturbance on habitat use by black-tailed godwits *Limosa limosa*. Journal of Applied Ecology. 38:846-856.

Annotation: Disturbance studies usually record short-term behavioral responses or compare animal distribution among sites having different disturbance levels. However, this study measured black-tailed godwit (*Limosa limosa islandica*) consumption of available food resources over the course of a winter at sites along the English coast having different levels of human activity. At each of three spatial scales (patch, mudflat, estuary), godwit use of a site was strongly correlated with the initial prey density in autumn. Godwit use of a site or remaining prey density at winter's end was not correlated with human activity levels. While some species may temporarily avoid human activities, the overall number of animals supported in an area may be unaffected by human activity.

Götmark, Frank; Neergaard, Raimo; Åhlund, Matti. 1989. Nesting ecology and management of the Arctic loon in Sweden. Journal of Wildlife Management. 53(4):1025-1031.

Annotation: On two Swedish lakes, the reproductive success of 20 pairs of breeding Arctic loons (*Gavia arctica*) was recorded before and after the closure of most nesting islands to public access. The mean annual production of young per territorial pair increased from 0.08 to 0.38 after the sanctuaries were established. In addition, hatching success increased on sanctuary islands but not on unprotected islands. Individual flushing distances in response to research boats approaching the nest were highly variable but averaged about 200 m. In some cases, flushed loons did not return to the nest for over one hour. Although the authors believed that disturbance influenced loon nesting success, a high water level in one of the 2 years preceding sanctuary establishment contributed to the low nesting success observed that year.

Henson, Paul; Grant, Todd A. 1991. The effects of human disturbance on trumpeter swan breeding behavior. Wildlife Society Bulletin. 19(3):248-257.

Annotation: On Alaska's Copper River Delta, six trumpeter swan (*Cygnus buccinator*) nests were observed over two seasons to assess the effects of human disturbance on nesting behavior. Regular aircraft overflights and road traffic alerted swans but did not cause incubating females to leave the nest. In contrast, stopped vehicles, pedestrians, and researchers prompted frequent recesses by incubating females. Whereas undisturbed swans always covered eggs with vegetation before leaving the nest, disturbed swans usually did not. Females also took longer recesses when disturbed and spent more time in an alert posture and less time feeding and preening. If frequent enough, these responses could lead to decreased egg and hatchling survival.

Keller, Verena. 1989. Variations in the response of great crested grebes *Podiceps cristatus* to human disturbance—a sign of adaptation? Biological Conservation. 49:31-45.

Annotation: In Switzerland, breeding great crested grebes (*Podiceps cristatus*) were observed on three lakes receiving different amounts of recreational use (nonmotorized boating, fishing, swimming). One privately owned lake received almost no recreational use, whereas the other two publicly owned lakes received frequent use. Compared to birds on the private lake, birds on the public lakes tolerated a much closer approach by rowboats or pedestrians before leaving their nest. This increased tolerance may allow some pairs to successfully breed on lakes with recreation. Nonetheless, overall nesting success was lower on the lakes with recreation. On these lakes, birds covered their eggs less frequently when leaving the nest, leaving the eggs exposed to potential predators.

Knapton, Richard W.; Petrie, Scott A.; Herring, Garth. 2000. Human disturbance of diving ducks on Long Point Bay, Lake Erie. Wildlife Society Bulletin. 28(4):923-930.

Annotation: During spring and fall migration, the authors monitored the responses of diving ducks (mainly *Aythya* spp.) to boating activity. The total number of birds that responded to disturbance was much higher in the fall when birds were concentrated into large flocks within no-hunting zones. All of the birds in these large flocks often took flight when approached by boats. In the fall, birds often discontinued their feeding, whereas birds disturbed in the spring quickly resumed feeding. However, springtime disturbances may be more harmful because females have a limited amount of time to accumulate the energy reserves needed for reproduction. The authors suggested that boat-free refuges be established during peak migration periods in both seasons.

Lafferty, Kevin D. 2001. Disturbance to wintering western snowy plovers. Biological Conservation. 101(3):315-325.

Annotation: Western snowy plovers (*Charadrius alexandrinus nivosus*) wintering on California beaches were observed to determine the effects of human disturbance. The beaches were closed to vehicles but were used by pedestrians (with and without dogs) and horse riders. Wintering plovers generally flushed when approached within 40 m, which is about half the initial flight distance reported for breeding plovers. Plovers were more likely to fly from dogs and horses than from people. The author developed a model to estimate the effectiveness of various management options. Prohibiting dogs and establishing a small buffer zone would eliminate over 90 percent of the disturbance events.

Liley, Durwyn; Sutherland, William J. 2007. Predicting the population consequences of human disturbance for Ringed Plovers *Charadrius hiaticula*: a game theory approach. Ibis. 149(Suppl. 1):82-94.

Annotation: See section II.C.2. Page 20.

Madsen, Jesper; Fox, Anthony D. 1995. Impacts of hunting disturbance on waterbirds—a review. Wildlife Biology. 1(4):193-207.

Annotation: This review summarizes the current state of knowledge about the indirect, nonconsumptive effects of hunting on waterbird populations. Although the review specifically focuses on European waterbirds, most European species have close North American relatives. Most waterbird studies have focused on geese and dabbling ducks, whereas few have addressed protected species, waders, and diving ducks. Generally, initial flight distances approximately double after the onset of hunting seasons. Waterbirds also move away from heavily hunted areas, and turnover increases at staging sites where hunting occurs. Some species are likely to be more sensitive to hunting disturbance than others (for example, species having less available foraging time to compensate for disrupted foraging and increased energy expenditure). Although little is known about the indirect impacts of hunting at the population level, evidence indicates that the amount of energy reserves accumulated during fall and winter can impact reproduction.

Morton, John M. 1996. Effects of human disturbance on the behavior and energetics of nonbreeding sanderlings. Dissertation, Blacksburg, VA, Virginia Polytechnic and State University.

Annotation: In this dissertation, the author proposes that an energetic response to disturbance can be measured as increased existence metabolism (EM). He proposes an energetic response is accompanied by three behavioral responses: (1) increased energy intake compensating for increased EM, (2) habituation reducing EM, and (3) dispersal avoiding an EM increase. Using these metrics, the author proposes a model to quantify disturbance impacts on birds. The author used experiments on caged dunlins (*Calidris alpinus*) and sanderlings (*Calidris alba*) to test his proposed model. In sanderlings, he found EM was elevated by 7 percent in response to disturbance. The author also compared distribution of birds in the wild in areas of high disturbance to those in areas of low disturbance. He found that increased pedestrian traffic decreased sanderling presence by 45 percent, and bird densities in disturbed plots were 60 percent less than in undisturbed plots. Disturbed sanderlings spent 151 percent more time in flight, 177 percent more time in maintenance behaviors, and 42 percent less time roosting than non-disturbed sanderlings. The dissertation also contains extensive literature reviews of the effects of disturbance on birds and of approaches to studying disturbance in wildlife, especially birds.

Morton, John M.; Fowler, Ada C.; Kirkpatrick, Roy L. 1989. Time and energy budgets of American black

ducks in winter. Journal of Wildlife Management. 53(2):401-410.

Annotation: The authors assessed the behavior and energy expenditure of American black ducks (*Anas rubripes*) wintering in Virginia. Flocks disturbed by human activity spent less time feeding and more time moving and remaining alert. To compensate for disturbance, birds appeared to rest during the day at a wildlife refuge and to feed at night in nearby salt marshes. Human activity could impair black duck energy intake, leading to reduced winter survival and/or reduced energy reserves heading into the breeding season.

Rodgers, James A., Jr.; Smith, Henry T. 1997. Buffer zone distances to protect foraging and loafing waterbirds from human disturbance in Florida. Wildlife Society Bulletin. 25(1):139-145.

Annotation: See section III.E.1. Page 38.

Titus, James R.; VanDruff, Larry W. 1981. Response of the common loon to recreational pressure in the Boundary Waters Canoe Area, northeastern Minnesota. Wildlife Monographs. 79:1-59.

Annotation: Within the Boundary Waters Canoe Area Wilderness, recreational use and common loon (*Gavia immer*) reproductive success were monitored over two consecutive summers. Nesting loons on lakes with high recreational use responded less strongly to approaching boats, and some reproductive measures (for example, number of eggs per breeding pair) were not affected by recreational use. However, loons on lakes with high recreational use fledged significantly fewer young to 2 weeks of age. Nonetheless, comparison with a previous study indicated that the loon population apparently increased over a 25-year period despite a concurrent, dramatic increase in recreation. The authors suggested that undisturbed breeding loons maintained the population. The authors recommended prohibiting campsites on islands, which is where most loon nests were located.

F. SONGBIRDS

Studies of disturbance impacts on songbirds are less common than for raptors or waterbirds. Studies focus on displacement from habitat (Blakesley and Reese 1988; Camp and Knight 1998; Gutzwiller and Anderson 1999), nest success or nest predation rates (Miller and Thompson 2000; Miller and others 1998; Westmoreland and Best 1985), and initial flight distances (Blumstein and others 2005; Fernández-Juricic and others 2005; Gutzwiller and others 1998). The experimental studies conducted by Gutzwiller and others (1998) and Gutzwiller and Anderson (1999) are notable for their 5-year duration.

Blakesley, Jennifer A.; Reese, Kerry P. 1988. Avian use of campground and noncampground sites in riparian zones. Journal of Wildlife Management. 52(3):399-402.

Annotation: In northern Utah, the use of riparian habitat by 14 avian species was compared between campground and noncampground locations. A multivariate analysis of variance indicated a significant difference between the two avian communities. Seven species were associated with campgrounds, while six others were associated with noncampground sites. However, when the abundances of each species were compared between the two locations, none of the differences were significant. Differences in shrub/sapling and tree density, amount of deadwood, and litter depth between site types may have influenced avian distributions. Species nesting on or close to the ground were associated with noncampground sites, whereas species nesting in trees were associated with campgrounds. Some species may also be more sensitive to the presence of humans in campgrounds.

Blumstein, Daniel T.; Fernández-Juricic, Estaban; Zollner, Patrick A.; Garity, Susan C. 2005. Inter-specific variation in avian responses to human disturbance. Journal of Applied Ecology. 42:943-953.

Annotation: In an effort to help managers focus on more than one species at a time, this literature review describes patterns of anti-predator behavior across 150 bird species. This information helps managers and researchers make predictions about responses of groups of species to human disturbance. The authors reviewed research on avian alert distance across species and found that larger species had greater flight initiation and alert distances. Larger species also moved farther away and to less disturbed areas than smaller species. Based on their review, the authors recommend consideration of body size when designating human visitation levels and buffer zones for minimizing disturbance to birds. The authors also offer three recommendations for predicting the response of different bird species to human disturbance: (1) study multiple indicators of disturbance stress and select those with lowest variation among individuals of the same species, (2) identify species-specific responses, and (3) assess how species-specific responses correlate with biological characteristics such as life history and natural history traits.

Camp, Richard J.; Knight, Richard L. 1998. Rock climbing and cliff bird communities at Joshua Tree National Park, California. Wildlife Society Bulletin. 26(4):892-898.

Annotation: In this study, bird communities differed among cliffs receiving different amounts of rock climbing. For instance, four species were found only near cliffs with no climbing, five were observed only near cliffs with moderate levels of climbing, and three were seen only near popular climbing cliffs. Brown-headed cowbirds (*Molothrus ater*), European starlings (*Sturnus vulgaris*), and house finches (*Carpodacus mexicanus*) were closely associated with climbed cliffs, possibly because these cliffs were closer to campgrounds and parking lots. Birds at unclimbed cliffs were more likely to be perched on the cliff face, whereas birds at climbed cliffs were more likely to be flying and located farther from the cliff face.

Fernández-Juricic, Estaban; Venier, M. Paula; Renison, Daniel; Blumstein, Daniel T. 2005. **Sensitivity of wildlife to spatial patterns of recreationist behavior: A critical assessment of minimum approaching distances and buffer areas for grassland birds.** Biological Conservation. 125:225-235.

Annotation: See section IV.B.2. Page 56.

Foin, T. C.; Garton, E. O.; Bowen, C. W.; Everingham, J. M.; Schultz, R. O.; Holton, B., Jr. 1977. **Quantitative studies of visitor impacts on environments of Yosemite National Park, California, and their implications for Park management policy.** Journal of Environmental Management. 5:1-22.

Annotation: See section III.C.1. Page 32.

Gutzwiller, Kevin J.; Anderson, Stanley H. 1999. **Spatial extent of human-intrusion effects on subalpine bird distributions.** Condor. 101(2):378-389.

Annotation: Within a Wyoming mixed-conifer forest, the authors used an experimental approach to assess the spatial extent of the effects of human intrusion on avian distributions. Over a period of 5 years, solitary hikers walked throughout experimental plots for 1 to 5 hours each week for 10 consecutive weeks during the breeding season. In most cases, species abundances were similar between experimental and control sites. Mountain chickadees (*Parus gambeli*) were less abundant at experimental sites for 2 of the years. American robin (*Turdus migratorius*) and hermit thrush (*Catharus guttatus*) were less abundant at experimental sites in the first year only. The researchers were able to detect birds located outside of the 100-m radius experimental plot as well, and species' abundances outside of the plot did not differ significantly between experimental and control sites. Thus, effects due to human intrusion were infrequent and limited to the actual site of the intrusion.

Gutzwiller, Kevin J.; Marcum, Heidi A.; Harvey, Henry B.; Roth, James D.; Anderson, Stanley H. 1998. **Bird tolerance to human intrusion in Wyoming montane forests.** Condor. 100(3):519-527.

Annotation: Over a 5-year period, five common passerine species were repeatedly approached by a solitary hiker to assess their tolerance for human presence and factors influencing their response. Responses varied significantly among years. The authors hypothesized that each year they encountered new individuals that had experienced different outcomes (positive, negative, neutral) in previous encounters with humans. Birds appeared to be less tolerant of human approach when in smaller groups. Additionally, species that were more conspicuously colored and active close to the ground were less tolerant of approach. Other factors found to be important in previous research, such as time of day and season, vegetation density, and species body mass, were not significantly related to response, demonstrating that tolerance can be species- and context-dependent.

Gutzwiller, Kevin J.; Riffell, Samuel K.; Anderson, Stanley H. 2002. **Repeated human intrusion and the potential for nest predation by gray jays.** Journal of Wildlife Management. 66(2):372-380.

Annotation: An experimental approach was used to test for the effects of human intrusion on gray jays (*Perisoreus canadensis*) within mixed-conifer forest in Wyoming. Over a period of 5 years, solitary hikers walked around in experimental plots for 1 to 2 hours each week for 10 consecutive weeks during the breeding season. During all 5 years, gray jay abundance and recurrence was higher on experimental sites than control sites, although the difference was significant only during the first 2 years. By attracting gray jays, relatively low levels of human intrusion may increase the potential for predation of songbird nests.

Mallord, John. W.; Dolman, Paul M.; Brown, Andy F.; Sutherland, William J. 2007. **Linking recreational disturbance to population size in a ground-nesting passerine.** Journal of Applied Ecology. 44: 185-195.

Annotation: See section II.C.2. Page 20.

Miller, James R.; Hobbs, N. Thompson. 2000. **Recreational trails, human activity, and nest predation in lowland riparian areas.** Landscape and Urban Planning. 50(4):227-236.

Annotation: Within a riparian corridor along Colorado's Front Range, artificial bird nests containing real and clay eggs were placed in three locations: next to trails, on the opposite side of the stream from trails, and at reference sites located far from trails. During the 2-year study, overall predation rates were high (94 percent). Daily predation rates increased with increasing distance from trails and during the second year. Whereas avian predators attacked more nests near trails, mammals appeared to avoid nests near trails. These results showed that trail effects on nest predation will depend on how trails influence the entire suite of nest predators at a particular location.

Miller, Scott G.; Knight, Richard L.; Miller, Clinton K. 1998. **Influence of recreational trails on breeding bird communities.** Ecological Applications. 8(1):162-169.

Annotation: In mixed-grass prairie and forest locations along Colorado's Front Range, bird species composition, nest predation, and brood parasitism by cowbirds (*Molothrus ater*) were examined at varying distances from recreational trails. Three grassland species and five forest species were significantly more abundant along control transects than near trails, whereas the American robin (*Turdus migratorius*) was more abundant near forest trails. Furthermore, grassland birds were less likely to nest near trails, and nest predation rates were higher near trails in both systems. Brood parasitism rates were not influenced by trails. The authors did not know whether trail effects occurred due to local habitat alteration or recreational disturbance.

Miller, Scott G.; Knight, Richard L.; Miller, Clinton K. 2001. **Wildlife responses to pedestrians and dogs.** Wildlife Society Bulletin. 29(1):124-132.

Annotation: See section III.B.1. Page 29.

Riffell, Samuel K.; Gutzwiller, Kevin J.; Anderson, Stanley H. 1996. Does repeated human intrusion cause cumulative declines in avian richness and abundance? Ecological Applications. 6(2):492-505.

Annotation: See section II.C.3. Page 21.

Westmoreland, David; Best, Louis B. 1985. The effect of disturbance on mourning dove nest success. Auk. 102(4):774-780.

Annotation: In an Iowa state park, mourning dove (*Zenaida macroura*) nest success was compared between experimentally disturbed and undisturbed nests. The experimental disturbance consisted of flushing birds from the nest every 3 days throughout the nesting period. Disturbed nests had lower daily survival probabilities than undisturbed nests, and this effect was most pronounced during the incubation period. However, nest-site variables that can affect nesting success (for example, nest height, depth, and concealment) differed between disturbed and undisturbed nests. Diurnal avian predators caused most nest failures at this site and may have observed nests from which attending adults were flushed.

G. REPTILES AND AMPHIBIANS

Studies of recreation impacts on reptiles and amphibians are rare, but existing studies indicate that recreation can affect some species. Garber and Burger (1995) document a long-term turtle population decline that coincided with the onset of recreational use. Other studies document recreation impacts on critical habitat (Goldingay and Newell 2000; Hosier and others 1981; Vinson 1998), behavior (Jacobson and Lopez 1994; Leuteritz and Manson 1996; Parent and Weatherhead 2000), and physiology (Romero and Wikelksi 2002).

Garber, Steven D.; Burger, Joanna. 1995. A 20-yr study documenting the relationship between turtle decline and human recreation. Ecological Applications. 5(4):1151-1162.

Annotation: Two reproductively isolated North American wood turtle (*Clemmys insculpta*) populations on a Connecticut preserve were monitored for 20 years. During the first 9 years of the study, both populations were stable. Over the next 11 years, both populations rapidly declined toward extinction. The declines coincided with the opening of the preserve to hiking and fishing. The authors considered alternate explanations for the declines (for example, air and water quality) and concluded that recreational use was the probable cause.

Goldingay, Ross L.; Newell, David A. 2000. Experimental rock outcrops reveal continuing habitat disturbance for an endangered Australian snake. Conservation Biology. 14(6):1908-1912.

Annotation: In Royal National Park near Sydney, Australia, the endangered broad-headed snake (*Hoplocephalus bungaroides*) requires small rock outcrops for shelter during the cooler months. The authors placed natural-appearing rock outcrops at various distances from roads and hiking trails to assess whether park visitors disturbed the snake's habitat. Over a 15-month period, rocks were overturned, smashed, or removed at 8 of the 22 outcrops. Disturbances occurred up to 450 m from the nearest road or trail. Thus, the authors recommended that habitat restoration efforts should be focused on sites at least 500 m from a road or trail.

Hosier, Paul E.; Kochhar, Medha; Thayer, Victoria. 1981. Off-road vehicle and pedestrian track effects on the sea-approach of hatchling loggerhead turtles. Environmental Conservation. 8(2):158-161.

Annotation: The authors experimentally tested the effects of off-road vehicle and pedestrian tracks on the ability of hatchling loggerhead turtles (*Caretta caretta caretta*) to navigate across North Carolina beaches and reach the ocean. Hatchling movement rates were significantly lower on beaches with vehicle or pedestrian tracks than on control beaches. Surface irregularities caused 21 percent of the experimental turtles to fall onto their backs; sometimes turtles required over 4 minutes to right themselves. The extended amount of time required to negotiate heavily used beaches may increase the susceptibility of hatchlings to predation and stress.

Jacobson, Susan K.; Lopez, Alfredo Figueroa. 1994. Biological impacts of ecotourism: tourists and nesting turtles in Tortuguero National Park, Costa Rica. Wildlife Society Bulletin. 22(3):414-419.

Annotation: Green sea turtle (*Chelonia mydas*) nesting activities were monitored on beaches that ecotourists visited to view the turtles. Fifty percent more turtles came onto the beach on weekday nights (when few people were present) than on weekend nights (when up to 90 people were present). The percentages of different nesting outcomes (nesting, false nesting, non-nesting) for individual turtles were similar on weekday and weekend nights. A successful guide program was later established by Park managers to minimize tourist impacts on nesting turtles.

Leuteritz, Thomas E.; Manson, Cynthia J. 1996. Preliminary observations on the effects of human perturbation on basking behavior in the midland painted turtle (*Chrysemys picta marginata*). Bulletin of the Maryland Herpetological Society. 32(1):16-23.

Annotation: In Michigan, midland painted turtle (*Chrysemys picta marginata*) basking behavior was compared between an undisturbed lake and a lake receiving pedestrian and motor vehicle use along the shoreline. Lake size and water temperature were similar for the two lakes, and logs were placed in the water at both lakes to provide a similar range of basking sites. At the disturbed lake, turtles basked significantly farther from the shore and were much less tolerant of human approach. Restricted or interrupted basking could affect turtle energy intake because thermoregulation is essential to food digestion.

Parent, C.; Weatherhead, P. J. 2000. Behavioral and life history responses of eastern massasauga rattlesnakes (*Sistrurus catenatus catenatus*) to human disturbance. Oecologia. 125(2):170-178.

Annotation: At Killbear Provincial Park in Ontario, Canada, eastern massasauga rattlesnakes (*Sistrurus catenatus catenatus*) were radiotracked to assess their behavioral responses to human activity. One study location was remote and rarely visited by people, whereas the other location was near a hiking trail, campsites, and roads. No differences in physical condition, growth rates, or female litter size were observed among snakes in the disturbed and undisturbed locations. However, snakes at the disturbed site moved less frequently and for shorter distances, possibly to remain hidden from nearby humans. A previous study found significant population genetic structure at a scale of less than 2 km, suggesting that recreation may have restricted gene flow within the population.

Prior, Kent A.; Weatherhead, Patrick J. 1994. Response of free-ranging eastern massasauga rattlesnakes to human disturbance. Journal of Herpetology. 28(2):255-257.

Annotation: The behavioral responses of eastern massasauga rattlesnakes (*Sistrurus catenatus catenatus*) to close approach by a hiker were studied at Bruce Peninsula National Park, Ontario, Canada. The snakes were exposed to three treatments: (1) hiker passed by at a distance of 0.5 m, (2) hiker remained at a distance of 0.5 m for 30 seconds, and (3) hiker stepped directly over the snake. No differences were apparent among the three treatments, and snakes showed no reaction in about 60 percent of the trials. Response rate was positively correlated with body temperature, suggesting that disturbed snakes are more likely to remain stationary at colder temperatures.

Romero, Michael L.; Wikelski, Martin. 2002. Exposure to tourism reduces stress-induced corticosterone levels in Galapagos marine iguanas. Biological Conservation. 108(3):371-374.

Annotation: The authors studied the physiological effects of ecotourism on Galápagos marine iguanas (*Amblyrhynchus cristatus*) by measuring blood plasma levels of corticosterone, the hormone regulating the long-term stress response. Chronically high corticosterone levels, which might result from excessive human disturbance, can adversely affect reproduction and survival. Initial corticosterone levels were nearly identical, however, for an iguana group heavily exposed to ecotourism and a group at an unvisited site, suggesting that the exposed group had habituated to human presence. Both groups also exhibited elevated corticosterone levels after 30 minutes of capture and restraint, indicating a functioning physiological stress response, although the exposed group had a smaller response. A dampened stress response may not necessarily be beneficial if an animal is faced with a life-threatening stressor.

Vinson, Meg. 1998. Effects of recreational activities on declining anuran species in the John Muir Wilderness, CA. Missoula, MT: University of Montana. 83 p. Thesis.

Annotation: The author presented evidence that anurans (frogs and toads) at high-elevation lakes are adversely impacted by recreational use and its associated riparian habitat modification. Amphibian populations in the Sierra Nevada have seriously declined in this century, and increasing recreational use is a potential cause that has been largely overlooked. In this study, a number of recreational use and habitat variables were measured at sites around 51 lakes. Anurans were present at 24 of the lakes. Comparisons were then made at two scales: (1) between lakes where a given species was present and lakes at a similar elevation where the species was absent and (2) between anuran sites and random sites at the same lake. At both scales, anurans were less abundant in areas heavily used by horsepackers and backpackers. These areas contained greater amounts of bare ground. Although anuran abundance was greatly reduced at lakes containing fish, anuran distribution throughout the study area was not correlated with stocked fish distribution.

H. INVERTEBRATES

While many studies have been conducted of camping impacts on soil organisms (see Section II.D. *Indirect Impacts of Recreation on Wildlife Habitat*), studies of recreation impacts on other invertebrates are rare. Existing studies document trampling impacts on species diversity (Duffey 1975), community composition (Ghazanshahi and others 1983, Povey and Keough 1991), and the abundance of individual species (Steiner and Leatherman 1981, Wright and Li 1998). These studies have occurred in a wide range of habitats including ocean coasts, streams, grasslands, and rock climbing cliffs.

Duffey, Eric. 1975. The effects of human trampling on the fauna of grassland litter. Biological Conservation. 7:255-274.

Annotation: The author measured invertebrate abundance in grassland litter samples exposed to trampling over a period of 12 months. Taxonomic groups found in the samples included beetles, spiders, snails, and earthworms. For most taxonomic groups, control samples contained many more individuals and species than those exposed to trampling. The invertebrate fauna were not significantly different between the two levels of trampling intensity. Overall, the invertebrate fauna of grasslands appeared to be affected by levels of trampling much lower than those required to alter the structure and composition of the plant community.

Ghazanshahi, Jamshid; Huchel, Thomas D.; Devinny, Joseph S. 1983. Alteration of southern California rocky shore ecosystems by public recreational use. Journal of Environmental Management. 16(4):379-394.

Annotation: The algal and marine invertebrate communities were compared among nine rocky shoreline sites with different levels of pedestrian use. Although overall species diversity was not correlated with recreational use, changes in community composition were detected. At higher use levels, algae were generally reduced by trampling. Animal species that compete with algae for space, such as limpets and mussels, often increased with higher use. Certain species of algae and animals were more affected than others. Management guidelines were offered for determining whether to concentrate use in a few areas or to disperse use evenly over the entire area. Increased public education was suggested as a means of minimizing visitor impacts.

McMillan, Michele A.; Nekola, Jeffrey C.; Larson, Douglas W. 2003. Effects of rock climbing on the land snail community of the Niagara Escarpment in southern Ontario, Canada. Conservation Biology. 17(2):616-621.

Annotation: Land snail surveys were conducted at climbed and unclimbed sites in a popular rock-climbing region. Rock climbing may particularly affect land snails because land snail diversity is often higher on limestone outcrops than other habitats. Individuals were collected from almost half the land snail species occurring in Ontario. Snail density, richness, and diversity were significantly lower within all three cliff habitats (edge, face, and base) sampled at climbed sites. Fourteen species were found significantly more often at unclimbed sites, whereas only one species was found more often at climbed sites. The authors recommended the inclusion of gastropods in conservation plans for protected areas containing cliffs.

Povey, Anna; Keough, Michael J. 1991. Effects of trampling on plant and animal populations on rocky shores. Oikos. 61(3):355-368.

Annotation: At Point Nepean National Park in Australia, changes to the intertidal algal and marine invertebrate communities were evaluated for three experimental trampling levels (high, low, and none). High- and low-intensity trampling severely damaged the *Hormosira banksii* algal habitat, resulting in the replacement of this species assemblage with bare rock and grazing molluscs. Most mollusc species were fairly resistant to trampling. Even after more than 400 days of recovery, *H. banksii* cover at high-intensity trampling sites was only 75 percent of the value at control sites. Thus, even short periods of intense trampling may lead to persistent, long-term changes in intertidal communities.

Steiner, Alan J.; Leatherman, Stephen P. 1981. Recreational impacts on the distribution of ghost crabs *Ocypode quadrata* Fab. Biological Conservation. 20(2):111-122.

Annotation: On Assateague Island in Maryland and Virginia, the authors estimated ghost crab (*Ocypode quadrata*) abundance on beaches subject to different recreational activities (undisturbed, pedestrians, off-road vehicles [ORV]). Crab densities were lowest on beaches used by ORVs and were highest on the pedestrian beach. Whereas ORVs harmed crabs by either directly killing them or indirectly altering the beach habitat, food scraps left by pedestrian users may have boosted crab numbers.

Wright, Kristopher K.; Li, Judith L. 1998. Effects of recreational activities on the distribution of *Dicosmoecus gilvipes* in a mountain stream. Journal of the North American Benthological Society. 17(4):535-543.

Annotation: Larval caddisfly (*Dicosmoecus gilvipes*) abundance and algal biomass was monitored along Oregon's Quartzville Creek, a Federally designated Wild and Scenic River. The caddisfly is an integral component of stream food webs. Sites with high human use (camping, fishing, gold-prospecting) had significantly lower caddisfly densities than sites with low use. Caddisfly larvae feed atop large rocks in the stream bed and are susceptible to physical disturbance. Algal biomass was not correlated with either caddisfly density or human activity. Prior to the study's second year, an unusually severe flood occurred, and the area was closed to the public. The flood significantly reduced caddisfly density and algal biomass across all sites. Human disturbance impacts on caddisfly abundance were small relative to those produced by the flood.

IV. MANAGING BACKCOUNTRY RECREATION IMPACTS ON WILDLIFE

A. MANAGEMENT STRATEGIES AND PLANNING FRAMEWORKS

Many strategic decisions about backcountry management address the conflict between recreational use and nature conservation (Cole 1993). Such decisions include which impact management techniques to use and when and where to use them (Anderson and others 1998; Cole and others 1987; Hammitt and Cole 1998; Leung and Marion 1999; Manning and Lime 2000; Manning and others 1996; Ream 1979), and whether to manage visitors and/or wildlife (Gutzwiller and Cole 2005; Jacobsen and Kushlan 1986; Ream 1979). In order to effectively manage backcountry areas for both recreationists and wildlife, managers need to understand both the biology of species and the psychology of recreationists (Duffus and Dearden 1990).

Recreation planners often use planning frameworks, many of which are variations of the Limits of Acceptable Change (LAC) framework (McCool and Cole 1998, Stankey and others 1985), to guide decisions about when and where to manage recreation impacts. Addressing multiple values, these frameworks usually include selecting indicators and standards and monitoring conditions of chosen standards. In addition to LAC, such planning frameworks include Adaptive Impact Management (AIM) (Riley and others 2003), Experience-based Recreation Management (EBM) (Manfredo 2002), Protected Area Visitor Impact Management (PAVIM) (Farrell and Marion 2002), Visitor Experience and Resource Protection (VERP) (U.S. Department of the Interior 1997), and Visitor Impact Management (VIM) (Vaske and others 1995). Several of these frameworks are reviewed by Gutzwiller and Cole (2005), Manning and Lime (2000), and McCool and Cole (1998). In a recent reference on management strategies and planning, Gutzwiller and Cole (2005) address the use of existing planning frameworks for managing recreational disturbances on wildlife and elucidate the primary steps that most frameworks share in common. Other authors that focus on applying such frameworks to wildlife management issues include Higginbottom (2003), Manfredo (2002), Belknap (1998), and Morin and others (1997). Several authors recommend an adaptive approach, where management

actions are designed to further understanding (Gutzwiller 1993, Macnab 1983).

1. Management Strategies

Anderson, Dorothy H.; Lime, David W.; Wang, Theresa L. 1998. Maintaining the quality of park resources and visitor experiences. St. Paul, MN: University of Minnesota, Department of Forest Resources, Cooperative Park Studies Unit. 134 p.

Annotation: This handbook provides recreation managers with a step-by-step process for identifying and defining unacceptable impacts, as well as a range of techniques for addressing these impacts. Although the process was developed for the National Park Service, managers within any organization may find it useful. The handbook contains three sections. The first section details the five-step decision process. The second section contains three worksheets intended for use during the decision process. The worksheets help managers to specify problems, select strategies and tactics, and implement the plan. The third section reviews five general management strategies (site management, rationing and allocation, regulations, deference and enforcement, and visitor education) and a range of tactics (techniques) to implement these strategies, similar to Cole and others (1987). The authors describe each tactic and list some of its attributes including costs to visitors, costs to management, and effectiveness. For example, for the strategy of regulating visitors, tactics include restricting access to specific locations (zoning), restricting or prohibiting certain activities, and limiting group size, stock use, or pets.

Cline, R.; Sexton, N.; Stewart, S.C. 2007. A human-dimensions review of human-wildlife disturbance: a literature review of impacts, frameworks, and management solutions. Open-File Report 2007-1111. U.S. Geological Survey. 88 p.

Annotation: In support of the U.S. Fish and Wildlife Service Refuge System's Comprehensive Conservation Planning (CCP) efforts, this report summarizes knowledge about the human dimensions of wildlife management. Following a brief overview of wildlife responses to recreation, the authors introduce theoretical concepts of human values, attitudes and norms, visitor education as a means to alter behavior, and recreational carrying capacity. They describe three planning frameworks used to apply carrying capacity indicators and standards and summarize contemporary management solutions as described by Anderson and others 1998 (see annotation in this section). The report concludes by listing information needs identified during an informal survey of refuge managers and biologists and providing an annotated bibliography of approximately 50 publications.

Cole, David N. 1993. Minimizing conflict between recreation and nature conservation. In: Smith, D. S.; Hellmund, P. C., eds. Ecology of greenways: design and function of linear conservation areas. Minneapolis, MN: University of Minnesota Press: 105-122.

Annotation: The author offers strategies for reducing conflict when managing to provide recreational opportunities and conserve natural resources. After reviewing the ecological impacts of recreation, he discusses the characteristics of recreational use and environment that influence the amount of impact occurring at a specific site. He then reviews various strategies for minimizing recreational impacts. Direct methods can be employed, such as limiting the amount of use at a site by restricting visitor numbers. Conversely, indirect methods can be used, such as carefully locating and designing access points or educating visitors in hopes of influencing their behavior. The author notes that successful recreation management will usually require a combination of both approaches.

Cole, David N.; Petersen, Margaret E.; Lucas, Robert C. 1987. Managing wilderness recreation use: common problems and potential solutions. Gen. Tech. Rep. INT-230. Ogden, UT: U.S. Department of Agriculture, Forest Service, Intermountain Research Station. 60 p.

Annotation: This report contains a summary of management strategies and tactics to mitigate common wilderness recreation problems including wildlife impacts. The term "strategy" refers to a general management approach. The authors suggest seven strategies. The most relevant to managing for wildlife impacts are reducing the use of problem areas, modifying the location of use within problem areas, modifying the timing of use, and modifying the type of use and visitor behavior. Under each strategy, a number of specific management techniques (tactics) are offered for implementing the strategy. The authors describe each tactic in detail including its existing usage, costs to visitors and management, and effectiveness. For a number of specified recreation impacts, recommended strategies and tactics are presented. Wildlife impacts are subdivided into: (1) unintentional harassment of large mammals and birds, (2) competition for forage between recreational stock and wildlife, and (3) attraction of animals, such as bears, rodents, and jays, through feeding or improper food storage. As an example, one suggestion for reducing wildlife harassment is to modify the timing of use (strategy) by charging fees when disturbance potential is high (tactic).

Duffus, David A.; Dearden, Philip. 1990. Nonconsumptive wildlife-oriented recreation: a conceptual framework. Biological Conservation. 53(3):213-231.

Annotation: The number of people engaging in nonconsumptive, wildlife-oriented recreation has greatly increased in recent years, requiring a greater emphasis on managing nongame wildlife species. Nonconsumptive wildlife use consists of three elements: the focal species or species group, human user, and history of the relationship between the two. Accordingly, nonconsumptive wildlife management requires a biological understanding of species and their habitats, as well as a psychological understanding of human recreationists. As the number of visitors to a wildlife viewing site increases over time, the user group will become increasingly dominated by users having less preexisting knowledge of the area. Based on the current level of knowledge and skill displayed by visitors, managers may thus be able to foresee potential increases in visitation.

Glaspell, Brian; Puttkammer, Annette. 2001. Linking wilderness research and management—volume 2. Defining, managing, and monitoring wilderness visitor experiences: an annotated reading list. (Wright, Vita, series ed.) Gen. Tech. Rep. RMRS-GTR-79-VOL 2. Fort Collins, CO: U.S. Department of Agriculture, Forest Service, Rocky Mountain Research Station. 29 p.

Annotation: Recognizing that experiential opportunities are an important component of wilderness designation and that the relationship between use numbers and visitor experiences is complex, this publication provides an overview of the literature related to defining, managing, and monitoring visitor experiences in wilderness. This volume includes readings that address wilderness values, how to measure and describe wilderness experiences, influences to visitor experiences and visitor satisfaction, visitor management techniques, and wilderness management planning. The last section addresses planning frameworks, including carrying capacity, limits of acceptable change (LAC), visitor impact management (VIM), and visitor experience and resource protection (VERP), that can be used to ensure that quality wilderness experiences continue to be available for people with a variety of values. This section also includes reading lists on how to identify indicators, set standards, and monitor visitor experiences, all of which could be easily adapted to managing recreation impacts on wildlife.

Gutzwiller, Kevin J. 1993. Serial management experiments: an adaptive approach to reduce recreational impacts on wildlife. Transactions of the North American Wildlife and Natural Resources Conference. 58:528-536.

Annotation: Field experiments are needed to determine cause-and-effect relationships between recreational disturbance and wildlife impacts. Unfortunately, such experiments can be expensive or difficult to conduct. Thus, the author urges that recreation management be used to perform large-scale field experiments with different management actions corresponding to experimental treatments (factors). To obtain experimental units that are true controls, temporary closure of an area or the banning of certain activities may be necessary. Initially, repeated experiments should be conducted using multiple factors at a few coarse treatment levels to identify the most important factors and their range of greatest influence. Later experiments can be refined using finer levels of the important factors. This approach is illustrated using two hypothetical case studies.

Gutzwiller, Kevin J.; Cole, David N. 2005. Assessment and management of wildland recreational disturbance. In: Braun, Clait E., ed. Techniques for wildlife investigations and management. Sixth edition. The Wildlife Society: Bethesda, MD: 779-796.

Annotation: See section II.B. Page 16.

Hammitt, William, E.; Cole, David N. 1998. Management alternatives. Part V (Chapters 10-13) In: Wildland recreation: ecology and management. Second Edition John Wiley and Sons, Inc.: 205-347.

Annotation: Whereas earlier parts of this textbook introduce the concept of wildland recreation and provide overviews of recreation impacts on soil, vegetation, wildlife, and water, Part V (Chapters 10 through 13) focuses on management alternatives used to reduce and mitigate ecological impacts. Chapter 10 introduces planning frameworks, strategies, and types of management approaches. Chapter 11 discusses monitoring recreational impacts. Chapter 12 reviews visitor management techniques, including use limits, length of stay, use dispersal and concentration, types of use, group size, education, seasonal limits, campfire management, and visitor information. Finally, Chapter 13 reviews site management techniques such as use location, permanent and temporary closures, spatial distribution, site hardening and shielding, and site rehabilitation. While examples in this book draw primarily from literature on campsite and trail impact and management, this section covers a variety of techniques that are useful for reducing recreational impacts on wildlife.

Jacobsen, Terri; Kushlan, James A. 1986. Alligators in natural areas: choosing conservation policies consistent with local objectives. Biological Conservation. 36(2):181-196.

Annotation: In natural areas containing species that pose a potential threat to human safety, managers are challenged to meet the requirements of both visitors and native wildlife. Using alligators (*Alligator mississippiensis*) in Everglades National Park as a case study, the authors evaluated three criteria for choosing an appropriate management strategy: threat to human safety, economic necessity, and the ecological value of the species. First, contrary to public perceptions, alligators in the Park were not a severe safety threat. Although there were 27 incidents of aggressive alligator behavior over an 11-year period, no human injuries occurred. Second, although alligators are harvested regionally for economic benefit, Parks are not dependent upon native wildlife for direct generation of income. In fact, such practices run counter to traditional National Park Service policy. Third, alligators serve important ecological

functions within the Everglades. Thus, visitor management, rather than wildlife management, was deemed to be the appropriate policy. The Park was urged to continue using techniques such as educational programs, access barriers to active nest sites, and law enforcement.

Leung, Yu-Fai; Marion, Jeffrey L. 1999. Spatial strategies for managing visitor impacts in national parks. Journal of Park and Recreation Administration. 17(4):20-38.

Annotation: This paper reviews spatial strategies for managing recreation impacts in parks and protected areas. Based on park management literature, spatial strategies are classified into four basic types. *Spatial segregation* shields sensitive resources and separates conflicting types of use. *Spatial containment* aims to minimize cumulative impacts by confining use to designated locations. A *spatial dispersal* strategy spreads visitors' use across large parts of the protected area in order to reduce frequency and intensity of disturbance in any one area. Careful attention to *spatial configuration* of trails and recreational facilities concentrates impacts in designated areas. Through a survey of 92 managers of parks with backcountry access, the authors collated information on when and how often these management strategies were used in the field. Examples were given from national parks to demonstrate the diversity of management strategies used and the flexibility in their implementation across spatial scales.

Macnab, John. 1983. Wildlife management as scientific experimentation. Wildlife Society Bulletin. 11(4):397-401.

Annotation: The authors (John Macnab is a collective pen name) state that wildlife managers can greatly advance scientific knowledge by treating management actions as manipulative experiments. Management decisions are often based on long-standing, but untested, ideas or assumptions. Managers should identify these assumptions and state them as hypotheses. Next, managers should follow the rules of experimental design by ensuring that management actions, or treatments, are replicated and include control treatments. Finally, the treatment effects should be measured and the results reported, particularly if the expected results are not achieved.

Manning, Robert E. 2007. Parks and carrying capacity: commons without tragedy. Island Press: Washington, DC. 313 p.

Annotation: In this book, Manning summarizes research on recreation carrying capacity in support of U.S. National Park Service management. Carrying capacity is generally defined as how much use can and should be accommodated. After a brief review of the roots of the carrying capacity concept, Manning describes Limits of Acceptable Change and related carrying capacity frameworks as well as characteristics of good indicators and standards. In the second section, he describes research approaches that inform carrying capacity decisions, including qualitative and quantitative surveys, normative theory and methods, visual research approaches, tradeoff analysis, and simulation modeling. The third section offers a variety of case studies of research designed to support carrying capacity analyses and management of specific Parks. Next, Manning describes and evaluates management strategies and a variety of direct and indirect management tactics, including information/education and use rationing/allocation. The book concludes with appendices of indicators and standards from various studies of parks and protected areas.

Manning, Robert E.; Ballinger, Nicole L.; Marion, Jeffrey; Roggenbuck, Joseph. 1996. Recreation management in natural areas: problems, practices, status and trends. Natural Areas Journal. 16(2):142-146.

Annotation: Managers of most National Park Service units with substantial backcountry resources and overnight visitation responded to a survey regarding the Park's recreation problems and management practices. Managers perceived wildlife impacts to be less serious than many other problems, such as trail erosion, trail proliferation, campsite impacts, and visitor crowding. A majority of managers used three practices for reducing wildlife impacts: instructing visitors not to feed wildlife, prohibiting pets from the backcountry, and instructing visitors to view wildlife from a distance. In addition, managers consistently considered four practices to be "highly effective" at reducing wildlife impacts when used: temporary closure of sensitive areas, regulation of food storage and facilities, provision of user education programs, prohibition or restriction of pets, and information workshops for commercial outfitters and guides. After reviewing three similar previous surveys of wilderness managers, the authors noted that the use of both direct and indirect management techniques has increased substantially since 1979.

Merigliano, Linda; Smith, Bryan. 2000. Keeping wilderness wild: increasing effectiveness with limited resources. In: Cole, David N.; McCool, Stephen F.; Borrie, William T.; O'Loughlin, Jennifer, comps. Wilderness science in a time of change conference—Volume 4: Wilderness visitors, experiences, and visitor management; 1999 May 23–27; Missoula, MT. Proceedings RMRS-P-15-VOL-4. Ogden, UT: U.S. Department of Agriculture, Forest Service, Rocky Mountain Research Station: 236-242.

Annotation: Traditionally, wilderness rangers have spent most of their time patrolling areas of high visitor use and impact. The authors argued, however, that priority should be given to areas of low visitor use and impact because these areas are most precious, vulnerable to change, and responsive to management action. Using attribute maps, the authors identified and prioritized management areas within Wyoming's Gros Ventre Wilderness. This Wilderness was designated primarily to protect elk and bighorn sheep habitat, unique geological features, and watersheds. Among these attributes, wildlife was thought to be at greatest risk to increasing levels of recreational use. Thus, a map of critical wildlife habitat was overlaid with a map delineating three levels of recreation and grazing impact (undisturbed, lightly disturbed, and disturbed) to generate five management priority zones. Greatest priority was given to areas of undisturbed, critical wildlife habitat. Wilderness rangers began spending more time in high-priority areas to document existing conditions and monitor changes in these conditions. This information was also used to locate future road improvements away from undisturbed areas.

Purdy, Ken G.; Goff, Gary R.; Decker, Daniel J.; Pomerantz, Gerri A.; Connelly, Nancy A. 1987. A guide to managing human activity on National Wildlife Refuges. Fort Collins, CO: U.S. Department of the Interior, Fish and Wildlife Service, Office of Information Transfer. 57 p.

Annotation: In this report, the authors propose a framework for managing recreational use on National Wildlife Refuges to reduce impacts on wildlife. They argue that the concept of "consumptive" and "nonconsumptive" use is invalid because activities such as wildlife observation, hiking, and boating can impact wildlife populations as much as hunting. Instead, managers should specify the types of impact associated with each activity and assess the most serious problems on the Refuge accordingly. Recommended impact categories are direct mortality, indirect mortality, lowered productivity, reduced use of the Refuge, reduced use of preferred habitat on the Refuge, and aberrant behavior/stress. In a survey conducted by the authors, Region 5 (Northeast) Refuge Managers reported that lowered productivity was the most common visitor impact, being cited as the primary impact in 41 percent of the situations where an impact occurred. The authors provide a table listing the reported impacts in Region 5 for a number of recreational activities, methods recommended by managers for mitigating each impact, and pertinent literature references.

Ream, Catherine H. 1979. Human-wildlife conflicts in backcountry: possible solutions. In: Ittner, Ruth; Potter, Dale R.; Agee, James K.; Anschell, Susie, eds. Recreational impact on wildlands—proceedings of a conference; 1978 October 27–29; Seattle, WA. Publ. No. R-6-001-1979. Portland, OR: U.S. Department of Agriculture, Forest Service, Pacific Northwest Region.

Annotation: Although difficult to document, unintentional harassment of wildlife may cause severe or irreversible damage before the problem is recognized. In support of this view, the author reviews studies documenting recreation impacts on birds, ungulates, and bears. Three general approaches to managing human-wildlife conflicts are then discussed: people management, wildlife management, and habitat management. Visitor education efforts should attempt to increase understanding of wildlife biology, and emphasize potential recreation impacts and appropriate behavior. Other suggested indirect methods for managing people include omitting bridges to keep people out of areas until high water (and calving season) has passed, terminating fish-stocking programs in certain alpine lakes, and leaving some areas trailless. Wildlife behavior may be modified so that animals become habituated to people in National Parks or conditioned to avoid people in areas that allow hunting. Finally, habitat can be manipulated (for example, using prescribed fire) to attract animals away from areas used by recreationists.

2. Formal Planning Frameworks

Belknap, Jayne. 1998. Choosing indicators of natural resource condition: a case study in Arches National Park, Utah, USA. Environmental Management. 22(4):635-642.

Annotation: Although many potential biological indicator variables have been identified for monitoring recreational impacts, this study demonstrated a process for choosing the best indicators at a specific location. Within the vegetation types most frequently used by Park visitors, vegetation and soil characteristics were sampled and compared between heavily and lightly used sites. Variables that differed significantly between sites were judged on a number of criteria, such as ecological relevance, impact to measure, reliability, and cost. Selected indicator variables were refined during additional field tests. Specific high-use sites were then selected for monitoring. Annual sampling was planned for indicators that were easy to measure, and sampling every 5 years was planned for indicators requiring more money or expertise to measure.

Farrell, Tracy A.; Marion, Jeffrey L. 2002. The Protected Area Visitor Impact Management (PAVIM) Framework: a simplified process for making management decisions. Journal of Sustainable Tourism. 10(1):31-51.

Annotation: The authors propose Protected Area Visitor Impact Management (PAVIM) as an alternative to Limits of Acceptable Change and other similar frameworks. Using PAVIM, managers collaborate with the public to identify an area's value, purpose, and management zones; specify management objectives; and identify and prioritize social and resource impact problems. An expert panel is then formed, composed of individuals having expertise relevant to the highest priority management problems. Experts can include local residents, agency representatives, scientists, and staff of nongovernment organizations. This panel conducts problem analyses, selects and implements management actions, and assesses the effectiveness of these actions. The PAVIM framework may be preferable if managers lack the funding, staffing, and time to conduct the data collection, analysis, and monitoring required by other frameworks. Although specifically developed from case studies in Central and South America, the authors suggest that PAVIM may also be effectively used in developed countries.

Hammit, William, E.; Cole, David N. 1998. Management alternatives. Part V (Chapters 10-13) In: Wildland recreation: ecology and management. Second Edition John Wiley and Sons, Inc.: 205-347.

Annotation: See section IV.A.1. Page 49.

Higginbottom, Karen; Green, Ronda; Northrope, Chelsea. 2003. A framework for managing the negative impacts of wildlife tourism on wildlife. Human Dimensions of Wildlife. 8:1-24.

Annotation: Using examples from Australian systems, Higginbottom and others offer a simple framework for setting up a program to manage wildlife tourism impacts on wildlife. They address how to choose appropriate overall management frameworks and management actions and how to design monitoring programs. Tables include: (1) components of the wildlife tourism system that can be managed, (2) approaches to managing the impacts of wildlife tourism on wildlife, (3) aspects of wildlife and habitat that can be monitored, (4) requirements of programs designed to monitor the impacts of tourism on wildlife, and (5) common problems associated with wildlife monitoring program and potential solutions.

Manfredo, Michael J., ed. 2002. Wildlife viewing: a management handbook. Corvallis, OR: Oregon State University Press. 373 p.

Annotation: This book covers a diverse range of topics related to wildlife viewing with an underlying emphasis on a management approach called Experience-based Recreation Management (EBM). Under the EBM model, people choose to participate in a particular recreation activity in a specific type of setting in order to attain certain desired psychological outcomes (in effect, experiences). The manager places equal emphasis on protecting wildlife and providing opportunities for recreationists to achieve their desired outcomes. In early chapters, authors discuss the increasing participation in wildlife viewing in North America and the important societal benefits provided by this pastime. Next, the fundamental concepts of the EBM approach are reviewed, an EBM planning framework is outlined, and methods for choosing indicators, standards, and management strategies are discussed. Later chapters review detailed techniques for wildlife management, economic valuation, visitor education, and marketing.

Manning, Robert E.; Lime, David W. 2000. Defining and managing the quality of wilderness recreation experiences. In: Cole, David N.; McCool, Stephen F.; Borrie, William T.; O'Loughlin, Jennifer, comps. Wilderness science in a time of change conference—Volume 4: Wilderness visitors, experiences, and visitor management; 1999 May 23–27; Missoula, MT. Proceedings RMRS-P-15-VOL-4. Ogden, UT: U.S. Department of Agriculture, Forest Service, Rocky Mountain Research Station: 208-216.

Annotation: The authors present a detailed review of planning frameworks and techniques for managing wilderness recreation. Planning frameworks are divided into two general categories: carrying capacity and the Recreation Opportunity Spectrum (ROS). Carrying capacity frameworks are based on the concept that a given area can sustain a specific amount of use before unacceptable impacts occur. These frameworks include Limits of Acceptable Change, Visitor Impact Management, and Visitor Experience and Resource Protection. The ROS framework emphasizes managing for a diversity of recreation settings, based on the assumption that a diverse range of experiences will then be available to the user constituency. Next, recommendations are given for choosing good indicators and standards to monitor user impacts based upon the research literature. The authors then review alternative wilderness recreation management techniques and their effectiveness. These techniques are divided into three main categories:

(1) information and education, (2) use rationing and allocation, and (3) other management practices. An extensive list of citations is provided in the References section.

McCool, Stephen F.; Cole, David N. comps. 1998. Proceedings—Limits of Acceptable Change and related planning processes: progress and future directions; 1997 May 20–22; Missoula, MT. Gen. Tech. Rep. INT-371. Ogden, UT: U.S. Department of Agriculture, Forest Service, Rocky Mountain Research Station. 84 p.

Annotation: Convened 12 years after the initial development of the Limits of Acceptable Change (LAC) process, this workshop was held to review and resolve issues encountered during implementation of LAC and similar processes. The Proceedings contain three sections: (1) invited papers discussing the original intent of the LAC process, lessons learned from its application, overcoming problems with the LAC process, the use of similar planning frameworks (VERP, VIM, VAMP) developed for agencies other than the Forest Service, and extending LAC's application to issues beyond wilderness recreation (for example, wildlife), (2) postsymposium synthesis papers summarizing the results of participant discussions, and (3) an annotated bibliography of references related to the LAC process.

Morin, Shannon L.; Moore, Susan A.; Schmidt, Wayne. 1997. Defining indicators and standards for recreation impacts in Nuyts Wilderness, Walpole-Nornalup National Park, Western Australia. CALMScience. 2(3):247-266.

Annotation: The authors surveyed Park visitors to determine the factors affecting their wilderness experience and quantify visitor tolerance for these factors. The survey results guided the development of monitoring indicators and standards for managing recreation in the Wilderness. Chosen indicators were amount of tree damage, vegetation loss, and litter; number and size of groups encountered; and number of signs. Standards were then developed meeting the tolerance level of at least 50 percent of the survey respondents (for example, no more than six groups encountered per day along trails). Although seeing wildlife was an important component of the visitor experience, wildlife-related indicators were not included because the authors considered wildlife presence and abundance to be largely beyond the control of managers.

Riley, Shawn J.; Siemer, William F.; Decker, Daniel J.; Carpenter, Len H.; Organ, John F.; Berchelli, Louis T. 2003. Adaptive impact management: an integrative approach to wildlife management. Human Dimensions of Wildlife. 8:81-95.

Annotation: The Adaptive Impact Management (AIM) framework is characterized by continual monitoring of indicators that measure progress toward stated goals and the refinement of management practices when goals are not being achieved. While traditional adaptive management has focused strictly on biological outcomes (for example, increasing the abundance of a species), AIM seeks to define objectives based on the input of stakeholder groups.

Stakeholder groups may consist of persons representing recreationists, tourism interests, wildlife scientists, and/or other parties. Suggestions for selecting appropriate representatives are given. Stakeholder groups cooperate with managers to set desired objectives, develop alternative conceptual models of the system, and identify management actions that consider the likelihood of each model. Progress toward achieving the desired objectives is then monitored and system models and management actions are adjusted accordingly. A case study is provided with the application of AIM to black bear (*Ursus americanus)* management in New York.

Stankey, George H.; Cole, David N.; Lucas, Robert C.; Petersen, Margaret E.; Frissell, Sidney S. 1985. The Limits of Acceptable Change (LAC) system for wilderness planning. Gen. Tech. Rep. INT-176. Ogden, UT: U.S. Department of Agriculture, Intermountain Forest and Range Experiment Station. 37 p.

Annotation: The authors detail the Limits of Acceptable Change (LAC) process for developing wilderness management plans, particularly with respect to recreation. This process has four major components: (1) specifying acceptable resource and social conditions, defined by measurable indicators, (2) determining the relationship between existing and desired conditions, (3) developing management actions necessary to achieve the desired conditions, and (4) instituting a monitoring program for evaluating management effectiveness. Suggested resource indicators include trail and campsite conditions, water quality, wildlife populations, and threatened or endangered species. Suggested social indicators include trail and campsite solitude and noise levels. A hypothetical example is provided to illustrate the use of LAC. After a decade of LAC implementation, a workshop was held to review and resolve issues regarding its implementation (see McCool and others 1997).

U.S. Department of the Interior, National Park Service. 1997. The Visitor Experience and Resource Protection (VERP) framework: a handbook for planners and managers. Denver, CO: Denver Service Center. 103 p. *(Note: This document can be downloaded at http://planning.nps. gov/document/verphandbook.pdf* [April 18, 2008])

Annotation: Developed for use by the National Park Service, the Visitor Experience and Resource Protection (VERP) framework shares the following elements with the Limits of Acceptable Change process: (1) description of the desired future conditions of Park resources and visitor experiences, (2) identification of specific indicators for these conditions, (3) establishment of standards that define minimum acceptable conditions, (4) development of indicator monitoring techniques, and (5) development of management actions to ensure that indicators are maintained within the specified standards. However, the VERP framework also contains preliminary steps such as the assembly of an interdisciplinary project team, development of a public involvement strategy, and articulation of Park purpose and significance. An example of its implementation is provided from Arches National Park. A bibliography is included containing references on other planning frameworks, public involvement strategies, indicators and standards, monitoring, and management actions.

Vaske, Jerry J.; Decker, Daniel J.; Manfredo, Michael J. 1995. Human dimensions of wildlife management: an integrated framework for coexistence. In: Knight, Richard L.; Gutzwiller, Kevin J., eds. Wildlife and recreationists: coexistence through management and research. Washington, DC: Island Press: 33-49.

Annotation: The authors review the Visitor Impact Management (VIM) process, which is similar to the Limits of Acceptable Change process. Using VIM, managers identify visitor impact problems (social and ecological), select indicators and standards for these impacts, and monitor the chosen indicators. If standards are not being met, managers identify the probable causes of noncompliance and alternative management strategies for reducing impacts. Alternative strategies are evaluated using a matrix of selection criteria including their consistency with management objectives and difficulty to implement. The authors encourage the use of multiple management techniques. A case study involving three Massachusetts nature preserves illustrates the use of the VIM process. These coastal preserves were established to protect shorebird populations and dune ecosystems while providing opportunities for a range of recreational activities.

Wilson, Steven F.; Hamilton, Dennis. 2005. A strategy to manage backcountry recreation in relation to wildlife and habitats. Biodiversity Branch, British Columbia Ministry of Environment: Victoria, BC. Available online at: http://www.env.gov.bc.ca/wld/twg/documents/wilson_hamilton_strategy.pdf [April 18, 2008].

Annotation: This strategy, an application of the planning frameworks addressed in this section, proposes a framework for managing backcountry recreation impacts on wildlife and wildlife habitat in British Columbia. Based on a general assessment of ecological risk, the authors recognize three management tools (prohibition, limits on user "inputs," and limits on "outcomes" guided by future desired conditions). For each management tool, the authors offer a brief description of the tool, its management intent, how it is best applied, its monitoring requirements, and its principle disadvantages. Then they describe a strategy for developing guidelines based on five broad habitat types (grassland, alpine/tundra, freshwater, coastal foreshore, forest) and five issue categories (for example, direct disturbance to wildlife) within each habitat type. The guidelines, which will be developed with input from commercial tourism operators, include desired future conditions, desired user behaviors, monitoring indicators, and tolerance limits for each habitat type and management issue. The authors recognize monitoring as a critical component of the strategy, describe the appropriate application of different monitoring levels, and differentiate between compliance and effectiveness monitoring. They conclude with a flowchart that includes the risk assessment, management tools, and monitoring levels. *(Note: This document was used to create the 2006*

Wildlife Guidelines for Backcountry Tourism/Commercial Recreation in British Columbia (available online at http://www.env.gov.bc.ca/wld/twg/index.html [April 18, 2008]).

B. MANAGEMENT TECHNIQUES

Managers use a variety of techniques to reduce recreation impacts (for overviews and comparisons, see Section IV.A. Management Strategies and Planning Frameworks). These include visitor education; visitor use restrictions and zoning; and trail, campsite, and road design. Several authors recommend using these techniques to protect wildlife (Burger 1995; Mace and Waller 1996; Merrill 1978; Stalmaster and Kaiser 1998; Taylor and Knight 2003). Publications specifically addressing visitor education discuss message content, such as low impact recreation practices (Cole 1989), techniques for communicating messages effectively (Cole and others 1997; Doucette and Cole 1993; McCool and Cole 2000; Roggenbuck 1992; Vander Stoep and Roggenbuck 1996) and information to help managers understand visitor non-compliance with management messages (Harding and others 2000, McCool and Brathwaite 1989).

Another technique, implementing visitor use restrictions and zoning, can be controversial and requires understanding existing visitor use patterns (Cole 2005, Jacobs and Schloeder 1992), influences to visitor experiences (Glaspell and Puttkammer 2001), and visitor support for restrictions (Frost and McCool 1988, Bultena and others 1981). Techniques used to restrict use (McCool and Christensen 1996) include buffer zones around wildlife locations (Camp and others 1997; Fernández-Juricic and others 2005; Lafferty 2001; Richardson and Miller 1997; Rodgers and Smith 1997; Rodgers and Smith 1995; Stalmaster and Kaiser 1998), use permits (Stankey and Baden 1977), cave gates (Ludlow and Gore 2000, White and Seginak 1987), and rock climbing restrictions (Pyke 1997).

Visitor use can also be indirectly managed through the design and location of trails, campsites, and roads within or adjacent to backcountry areas. Publications on this topic often explore the effects of these developments on wildlife (Blakesley and Reese 1988; Etchberger and others 1989; Fletcher and others 1999; Gaines and others 2003; Janis and Clark 2002; Kasworm and Manley 1990; Lacki 2000; Mace and Waller 1996; Miller and Hobbs 2000; Miller and others 1998; Thurber and others 1994; Whittington and others 2005). Additionally, some authors present guidelines or processes used to design trails (Trails and Wildlife Task Force, Colorado State Parks, Hellmund Associates 1998), campgrounds (Creachbaum and others 1998, Merrill 1978), and road pullouts (Montopoli and Anderson 1991) to minimize impacts on wildlife.

Some techniques directly target wildlife rather than people. Tools for managing bears include habituation (Aumiller and Matt 1994), aversive conditioning (Clark and others 2002), and bear-proof garbage and food storage facilities (Ingram 1994, Thompson and McCurdy 1994). Tools for managing birds include habituation (Nisbet 2000) and creating alternative habitat or habitat features in areas where such an approach is deemed appropriate (Burger 1995, McGarigal and others 1991). Habituation might also work for iguanas (Romero and Wikelski 2002).

1. Visitor Education

Cole, David N. 1989. Low-impact recreational practices for wilderness and backcountry. Gen. Tech. Rep. INT-265. Ogden, UT: U.S. Department of Agriculture, Forest Service, Intermountain Research Station. 131 p.

Annotation: The author describes 75 low-impact practices for backcountry recreation, as well as the rationale for each practice, its likely effectiveness, and sample messages for encouraging its use by recreationists. Several recommended practices are applicable to reducing wildlife disturbance. For example, off-trail travel may disturb animals that have sought out remote areas. A corresponding low-impact practice is for users to avoid off-trail travel unless prepared to use extra care with route selection, travel behavior, and campsite selection. Some recommended packstock practices, such as minimizing the number of stock and using supplemental weed-free feed, can reduce competition with wildlife for forage in heavily used areas. The author also discusses certain practices previously recommended by Federal agencies or other organizations that can actually be counterproductive or are appropriate only in specific situations.

Cole, David N.; Hammond, Timothy P.; McCool Stephen F. 1997. Information quantity and communication effectiveness: low-impact messages on wilderness trailside bulletin boards. Leisure Sciences. 19:59-72.

Annotation: The authors studied the effectiveness of trailside bulletin boards at gaining the attention of and communicating low-impact messages to wilderness visitors. The effect of information quantity and a message attractant was assessed by varying the number of messages from two to eight and by sometimes posting a map next to the messages. Seventy-one percent of hikers looked at the messages, as opposed to 27 percent of horse riders. Hikers exposed to the messages scored significantly higher on a low-impact quiz than hikers with no exposure. However, as the number of messages increased beyond two, the amount of time devoted to each message and the ability to retain message content decreased. Thus, quiz scores were not significantly different for hikers exposed to two messages and those exposed to eight messages. Posting a map had no effect on message attention or retention. Managers may be faced with selecting only a few critical messages designed to be processed in a short period of time. In addition, managers and researchers must find other means of communicating low-impact behavior to horse users.

Doucette, Joseph E.; Cole, David N. 1993. Wilderness visitor education: information about alternative techniques. Gen. Tech. Rep. INT-295. Ogden, UT: U.S. Department of Agriculture, Forest Service, Intermountain Research Station. 37 p.

Annotation: The authors summarize information on alternative techniques for educating wilderness visitors. In the first section, the results of a wilderness manager survey are presented. Managers described existing wilderness education methods and evaluated their cost and effectiveness. In the second section, the authors present a detailed description of each educational technique and important attributes, such as the amount of personnel time required for implementation, cost, effectiveness, advantages, and disadvantages. Techniques are classified as media-based (for example, signs, trailhead displays, and videos) or personnel-based (for example, personnel at visitor centers, trailheads, or in the backcountry). In the final section, innovative techniques and principles of effective wilderness education are discussed. An appendix contains an example of a high-quality wilderness education plan developed for the Mt. Shasta Wilderness in California.

Harding, James A.; Borrie, William T.; Cole, David N. 2000. Factors that limit compliance with low-impact recommendations. In: Cole, David N.; McCool Stephen F.; Borrie, William T.; O'Loughlin, Jennifer, comps. Wilderness science in a time of change conference—Volume 4: Wilderness visitors, experiences, and visitor management; 1999 May 23–27; Missoula, MT. Proc. RMRS-P-15-VOL-4. Ogden, UT: U.S. Department of Agriculture, Forest Service, Rocky Mountain Research Station: 198-202.

Annotation: Based on previous research, the authors speculate that lack of knowledge is not the only factor leading to wilderness visitors' noncompliance with low-impact techniques. Drawing on psychological theory, the authors outline four interconnected stages in the process of choosing whether to practice low-impact techniques. The outcome at any one of these stages can result in noncompliance. In the first stage ("interpretation of the situation"), the user must interpret site conditions and assess the need for low-impact behavior. During the second stage ("information retrieval strategies"), the user must retrieve information about a low-impact behavior from memory. In the third stage ("judgment formation"), the user assesses the importance of practicing the low-impact behavior. An individual's ethics play a large role in judgment formation. During the fourth stage ("expression of behavior"), the user decides whether to follow through with the low-impact behavior. Social pressure and the identity that the user wishes to portray to those around him are major influences at this stage. Persuasive strategies to change visitor behavior will be more effective if they target the factors that are contributing most to noncompliance at a specific location.

McCool, Stephen F.; Brathwaite, Amy M. 1989. Beliefs and behaviors of backcountry campers in Montana toward grizzly bears. Wildlife Society Bulletin. 17(4):514-519.

Annotation: Bear management plans rely heavily on persuading visitors to adopt recommended behaviors that reduce the chance of bear-human confrontations. In Glacier National Park and the Jewel Basin Hiking Area, backcountry campers were surveyed to assess the influence of their personal beliefs about bears on compliance with recommended camping practices. Both of these areas contain high densities of grizzly bears (*Ursus arctos horribilis*). Campers who believed that bears were essential components of the ecosystem and appreciated their existence were more likely to adopt safe camping practices. The authors suggest that information directed at increasing visitor sensitivity to the grizzly bear's ecological value may be more effective at encouraging safe camping practices than messages focused on safety hazards.

McCool, Stephen F.; Cole, David N. 2000. Communicating minimum impact behavior with trailside bulletin boards: visitor characteristics associated with effectiveness. In: Cole, David N.; McCool, Stephen F.; Borrie, William T.; O'Loughlin, Jennifer, comps. Wilderness science in a time of change conference—Volume 4: Wilderness visitors, experiences, and visitor management; 1999 May 23–27; Missoula, MT. Proceedings RMRS-P-15-VOL-4. Ogden, UT: U.S. Department of Agriculture, Forest Service, Rocky Mountain Research Station: 208-216.

Annotation: Due to reduced budgets and a resulting reduced field presence, wilderness managers have increasingly relied upon trailside bulletin boards to communicate low-impact messages to visitors. To improve understanding of this medium's effectiveness, the authors studied the association between various visitor characteristics and the amount of attention given to and knowledge gained from a trailside bulletin board. Hikers were much more likely to stop at the board than horse users (85 percent versus 30 percent). In addition, overnight users were more likely to stop than day users (73 percent versus 63 percent). The authors suggested that one reason for this finding was that the messages had greater personal utility for overnight hikers. On average, visitors stopping at the board spent 5 seconds attending to each message. Hikers stopping at the board scored much higher on a subsequent knowledge quiz than horse users stopping at the board (56 percent versus 15 percent). Mechanisms should be developed and evaluated for more effective communication of low-impact behaviors to horse users.

Roggenbuck, Joseph W. 1992. The use of persuasion to reduce resource impacts and visitor conflicts. In: Manfredo, Michael J., ed. Influencing human behavior: theory and applications in recreation, tourism, and natural resources management. Champaign, IL: Sagamore Publishing: 149-208.

Annotation: The author reviews the use of persuasive communication as a recreation management tool. After first reviewing the types of resource impacts and visitor conflicts that commonly occur, he provides a classification of undesirable behavior types and assesses the likelihood that persuasion can effectively change each behavior type. The behavior types are illegal, careless, unskilled, uninformed, and unavoidable actions. Next, the three primary routes to persuasion are discussed. Using applied behavior analysis, managers attempt to change visitor behavior through behavior prompts, manipulation of the environment, rewards,

or punishments. Using the central persuasion route, managers attempt to persuade visitors to incorporate a message's content into their existing belief systems. This approach is most commonly used because the learned behavior can be expected to recur in the future. In contrast, the peripheral persuasion route involves minimal or no effort to integrate the message content into the visitor's belief system. With this approach, visitors often take action based upon how attractive or expert a message source appears. Finally, the author reviews the literature and summarizes his general findings on the effectiveness of persuasion at changing visitor beliefs and intentions, encouraging visitors to select alternative recreation sites, and reducing visitor impacts.

Stalmaster, Mark V.; Kaiser, James L. 1998. Effects of recreational activity on wintering bald eagles. Wildlife Monographs. 137:1-46.

Annotation: See section III.D.1. Page 35.

Taylor, Audrey R.; Knight, Richard L. 2003. Wildlife responses to recreation and associated visitor perceptions. Ecological Applications. 13(4):951-963.

Annotation: See section III.B.3. Page 31.

Vander Stoep, Gail A.; Roggenbuck, Joseph W. 1996. Is your park being "loved to death?": using communications and other indirect techniques to battle the park "love bug." In: Lime, David W., ed. Congestion and crowding in the National Park System: guidelines for management and research. Misc. Publ. 86-1996. St.Paul, MN: University of Minnesota, Minnesota Agricultural Experiment Research Station: 85-132.

Annotation: The authors discuss the use of indirect approaches, mainly communication, to manage recreation resource impacts. Several theoretical models are presented that predict the influence of external and internal variables on human behavior. By better understanding the diverse motivations for human behavior, managers can develop more suitable strategies for their specific sites, audiences, and objectives. The authors then summarize previous research assessing the effectiveness of different indirect management techniques. Based on these results, they present several general guidelines for using communication as a management tool. For example, indirect techniques should be varied and possibly combined with direct techniques (restrictions, sanctions, surveillance) because visitors have diverse motives, perceptions, and experience. After the Literature Cited, additional readings are suggested.

2. Visitor Use Restrictions and Zoning

Bultena, Gordon; Albrecht, Don; Womble, Peter. 1981. Freedom versus control: a study of backpackers' preferences for wilderness management. Leisure Sciences. 4(3):297-310.

Annotation: The authors surveyed backcountry visitors to Denali National Park to determine their support for the Park's backcountry policies. The Park has a permit system that places strict rationing and camping controls on backcountry visitors. Eighty-five percent of respondents were opposed to permitting uncontrolled use levels in the backcountry. Among five alternatives, the only rationing policy supported by a majority of respondents (82 percent) was to issue a limited number of permits on a first-come, first-served basis. The other alternatives were to issue permits through an advance registration system, issue permits to those demonstrating a specified knowledge and skill level, charge a user fee, or issue permits through a lottery system. When questioned on their attitudes toward 13 existing Park backcountry regulations, a majority of respondents overwhelmingly supported each of the 13 regulations. The regulation getting the greatest support (93 percent) was the permanent closure of some areas to protect fragile wildlife habitats.

Burger, Joanna. 1995. Beach recreation and nesting birds. In: Knight, Richard L.; Gutzwiller, Kevin J., eds. Wildlife and recreationists: coexistence through management and research. Washington, DC: Island Press: 281-295.

Annotation: See section III.E.2. Page 39.

Camp, Richard J.; Sinton, David T.; Knight, Richard L. 1997. Viewsheds: a complementary management approach to buffer zones. Wildlife Society Bulletin. 25(3):612-615.

Annotation: To protect wildlife during sensitive time periods, such as with nesting raptors, managers commonly create spatial buffer zones around wildlife locations. Although the size of the buffer zone is based on observed flushing distances, animals may become agitated and respond physiologically prior to flushing. Thus, the authors suggest complementing spatial buffer zones with the use of viewsheds. Viewsheds are portions of the landscape that are visible from a point location. To demonstrate its application, the authors located golden eagle (*Aquila chrysaetos*) nests on cliffs within a Colorado nature preserve, rappelled to the nest sites, and obtained three-dimensional coordinates using a Global Positioning System unit. The viewshed from each nest site was then determined using Geographic Information System software and Digital Elevation Models. The viewshed area was three times greater than the area contained within previously suggested buffer zones. In areas containing more vegetation, the viewshed area could be less than that contained within buffer zones based on flush distance. By incorporating viewsheds into planning, managers may be better able to locate trails, panoramic sites, and tour routes.

Cole, David N., comp. 2005. Computer simulation modeling of recreation use: current status, case studies, and future directions. Gen. Tech. Rep. RMRS-GTR-143. Fort Collins, CO: U.S. Department of Agriculture, Forest Service, Rocky Mountain Research Station. 75 p.

Annotation: Emphasizing parks and wilderness, this report summarizes recent progress on computer simulation modeling for recreation use planning and management. Simulation models can be used to understand spatial and temporal visitor use patterns, predict how visitor distributions might change under different management scenarios, monitor hard-to-measure visitor use parameters, and communicate the implications of management options. Following the introduction and a chapter on the historical development of recreation use simulation models, the third chapter provides an overview of modeling options, common data input requirements, and model outputs. This is followed by a description of 12 case studies that demonstrate a variety of modeling situations and discuss the utility of model output for addressing questions about use levels and management consequences. The publication concludes with suggestions for future research in recreation simulation modeling.

Fernández-Juricic, Estaban; Venier, M. Paula; Renison, Daniel; Blumstein, Daniel T. 2005. Sensitivity of wildlife to spatial patterns of recreationist behavior: a critical assessment of minimum approaching distances and buffer areas for grassland birds. Biological Conservation. 125:225-235.

Annotation: This paper assesses the effects of direct and tangential approaches on grassland birds and evaluates methods commonly used to estimate buffer areas around sensitive wildlife habitat. The authors measured alert distances (AD) and flight initiation distances (FID) and compared these in response to human direct and tangential approaches. Contrary to other research, they found that four of the five species they studied had longer FIDs for tangential approaches than direct approaches. Based on the implication that FIDs may be used to determine buffer distances, the authors describe a robust method for estimating buffer zones that considers both FID and AD. However, since buffer zone requirements are highly dependent on the target species, the authors recommend concentrating the recreational visits spatially rather than designing a network of trails and buffer zones.

Frost, Jeffrey E.; McCool, Stephen F. 1988. Can visitor regulations enhance recreational experiences? Environmental Management. 12(1):5-9.

Annotation: Each fall, thousands of visitors to Montana's Glacier National Park view migrating bald eagles heavily concentrated along a salmon spawning stream. To protect the eagles from disturbance, Park managers restrict visitor access to a bridge across the stream or to a viewing blind in the company of a naturalist. Persons viewing the eagles were surveyed to determine their attitudes toward the Park's regulations. Among visitors who were aware of the restrictions, most believed that the restrictions had either no influence on their experience (56 percent) or actually facilitated their experience (32 percent). Furthermore, acceptance of the restrictions was more likely when visitors perceived the amount of information and the rationale provided as adequate. The authors noted that respondents were similar to wilderness visitors in terms of education, occupation, and age.

Glaspell, Brian; Puttkammer, Annette. 2001. Linking wilderness research and management—volume 2. Defining, managing, and monitoring wilderness visitor

experiences: an annotated reading list. (Wright, Vita, series ed.) Gen. Tech. Rep. RMRS-GTR-79-VOL 2. Fort Collins, CO: U.S. Department of Agriculture, Forest Service, Rocky Mountain Research Station. 29 p.

Annotation: See section IV.A.1. Page 48.

Hendee, John C.; Dawson, Chad P. 2002. Wilderness use and user trends. In: Hendee, John C.; Dawson, Chad P., eds. Wilderness management: stewardship and protection of resources and values. 3d ed. Golden, CO: Fulcrum Publishing: 373–411.

Annotation: This chapter begins with an overview of different types of wilderness use, including on-site recreation, use by non-visitors (such as ecological values), and scientific, educational, and allowable commodity uses. It reviews a variety of methods for estimating recreational use and user characteristics, describing the appropriate use, strengths, and weaknesses of each method. Next, the authors summarize wilderness recreation use trend studies, which have predominantly shown increases over the past 40 years. They describe various use (length of stay, travel method, activity, season, group size) and user (age, gender, residence, etc.) characteristics and the known geographical distribution of use. They conclude with a discussion of factors affecting use trends and then project continued increases in wilderness use.

Jacobs, Michael J.; Schloeder, Catherine A. 1992. Managing brown bears and wilderness recreation on the Kenai peninsula, Alaska, USA. Environmental Management. 16(2):249-254.

Annotation: The authors used electronic trail counters to estimate the number of hikers using a trail system traversing an area frequented by brown (Ursus arctos) and black bears (U. americanus). Trailhead questionnaires were used to collect information on human-bear encounters. The authors discussed problems they experienced with the trail counters and questionnaires and recommended some potential solutions. Although hikers reported no aggressive brown bear behavior during the 4-year period, the authors suggested that managers develop a formal management plan for the area using the Limits of Acceptable Change format (see Stankey and others 1985). The data collection techniques developed during this study could be used in future efforts to monitor human use and human-bear encounters.

Lafferty, Kevin D. 2001. Disturbance to wintering western snowy plovers. Biological Conservation. 101(3):315-325.

Annotation: See section III.E.2. Page 40.

Ludlow, Mark E.; Gore, Jeffery A. 2000. Effects of a cave gate on emergence patterns of colonial bats. Wildlife Society Bulletin. 28(1):191-196.

Annotation: See section III.C.2. Page 33.

McCool, Stephen F.; Christensen, Neal A. 1996. Alleviating congestion in parks and recreation areas through direct management of visitor behavior. In: Lime, David W., ed. Congestion and crowding in the National Park System: guidelines for management and research. Misc. Publ. 86-1996. St. Paul, MN: University of Minnesota, Minnesota Agricultural Experiment Research Station: 67-83.

Annotation: The authors distinguish between direct and indirect recreation management techniques. Direct methods rely on regulation of visitor behavior, while indirect methods emphasize providing information and education. Although managers generally prefer less intrusive, indirect methods in wilderness settings, direct methods often provide more protection to ecological resources. Based on published research, the authors summarize the frequency of use, costs, benefits, and general findings for a number of specific direct techniques. As an example, area closures have high costs to visitor freedom, yet visitors often support area closures if they understand the rationale for them. A list of research priorities for improving our knowledge of direct methods is then suggested.

Pyke, Kathryn. 1997. Raptors and climbers: guidance for managing technical climbing to protect raptor nest sites. Boulder, CO: The Access Fund. 26 p. (Note: This document can be ordered by contacting The Access Fund online at 303-545-6772.)

Annotation: This guide assists managers concerned with rock-climbing activities near cliff-nesting raptors. Climbing activity can impact raptor nests by altering habitat and disrupting foraging, nesting, and roosting behavior. The author provides an initial list of questions concerning the wildlife and recreation resources that will help managers assess the need for climbing restrictions. If restrictions are necessary, guidelines are provided for determining the size and seasonal timing of area closures. Appropriate media are suggested for alerting the rock-climbing community to current restrictions and providing information on the need for such restrictions. In particular, Access Fund representatives may be able to assist managers with the implementation of information and education programs at both the local and national level. An action plan for implementing a monitoring program is also provided. An appendix contains contact information for managers that have implemented climbing restrictions to protect nesting raptors.

Richardson, Cary T.; Miller, Clinton K. 1997. Recommendations for protecting raptors from human disturbance: a review. Wildlife Society Bulletin. 25(3):634-638.

Annotation: The authors advocate the use of spatial and temporal buffer zones to protect important raptor locations, such as nest sites, from human disturbance. For 11 raptor species, a literature summary of recommended buffer zones and initial flight distances is presented. When designing appropriate buffer zones, the most important factors to consider are site-specific physical characteristics, the source and duration of potential disturbances, and the prior disturbance history of individual birds. To ensure the success of buffer-zone restrictions, managers should employ visitor education and monitoring strategies.

Rodgers, James A., Jr.; Smith, Henry T. 1995. Setback distances to protect nesting bird colonies from human disturbance in Florida. Conservation Biology. 9(1):89-99.

Annotation: See section III.E.1. Page 38.

Rodgers, James A., Jr.; Smith, Henry T. 1997. Buffer zone distances to protect foraging and loafing waterbirds from human disturbance in Florida. Wildlife Society Bulletin. 25(1):139-145.

Annotation: See section III.E.1. Page 38.

Stalmaster, Mark V.; Kaiser, James L. 1998. Effects of recreational activity on wintering bald eagles. Wildlife Monographs. 137:1-46.

Annotation: See section III.D.1. Page 35.

Stankey, George H.; Baden, John. 1977. Rationing wilderness use: methods, problems, and guidelines. Res. Pap. INT-192. Ogden, UT: U.S. Department of Agriculture, Forest Service, Intermountain Forest and Range Experiment Station. 20 p.

Annotation: The authors discuss five alternative methods for rationing a limited number of wilderness use permits: advance reservations, lottery, queuing (first-come, first-served basis on or shortly before the permit date), price, and merit (requiring a demonstration of skill and knowledge). For each method, information is provided on the user groups that benefit or are adversely affected by it, its acceptability to users, its difficulty to administer, and its efficiency at allocating permits to persons placing the most value on a wilderness trip. The authors then describe five guidelines for rationing wilderness use: (1) accurate knowledge of existing resource impacts and the clientele is necessary, (2) rationing should only be used when less restrictive measures fail, (3) using a combination of methods will help minimize costs to both users and managers, (4) rationing should require users to judge the relative worth of the opportunity, and (5) monitoring and evaluation of the rationing program should be conducted.

White, Donald H.; Seginak, John T. 1987. Cave gate designs for use in protecting endangered bats. Wildlife Society Bulletin. 15(3):445-449.

Annotation: See section III.C.2. Page 33.

3. Design and Location of Trails, Campsites, and Roads

Blakesley, Jennifer A.; Reese, Kerry P. 1988. Avian use of campground and noncampground sites in riparian zones. Journal of Wildlife Management. 52(3):399-402.

Annotation: : See section III.F. Page 41.

Creachbaum, M. S.; Johnson, C.; Schmidt, R. H. 1998. Living on the edge: a process for redesigning campgrounds in grizzly bear habitat. Landscape and Urban Planning. 42:269-286.

Annotation: The authors recount a process used to redesign a popular National Forest campground in grizzly bear habitat in order to reduce the potential for bear-human conflicts. The campground was situated between Yellowstone National Park and two National Forest wilderness areas in Wyoming. Grizzly bear biologists and landscape architects convened for a 1-day session and were grouped into three planning teams. Each team incorporated their knowledge of bear habitat needs, behavior, and the causes of bear-human conflict into a proposed campground design. The three proposed campground designs shared many common elements, and design differences were resolved in a group discussion. The final design contained three distinct campground zones: (1) a centrally located community area where all food preparation, food storage, and garbage facilities were located, (2) a tent area located farthest from a bear travel corridor, and (3) a hard-sided camper area located closest to the bear corridor. Buffer zones, trails, and barriers were placed to route bears around the campground. The process and proposed design were endorsed by the U.S. Fish and Wildlife Service.

Etchberger, Richard C.; Krausman, Paul R.; Mazaika, Rosemary. 1989. Mountain sheep habitat characteristics in the Pusch Ridge Wilderness, Arizona. Journal of Wildlife Management. 53(4):902-907.

Annotation: See section III.B.2. Page 30.

Fletcher, Robert J., Jr.; McKinney, Shawn T.; Bock, Carl E. 1999. Effects of recreational trails on wintering diurnal raptors along riparian corridors in a Colorado grassland. Journal of Raptor Research. 33(3):233-239.

Annotation: See section III.D.2. Page 36.

Gaines, William L.; Singleton, Peter H.; Ross, Roger C. 2003. Assessing the cumulative effects of linear recreation routes on wildlife habitats on the Okanogan and Wenatchee National Forests. U.S. Department of Agriculture, Forest Service, Pacific Northwest Research Station. Gen. Tech. Rep. PNW-GTR-586. 79 p.

Annotation: The authors assessed the cumulative effects of linear recreation routes (roads, motorized and nonmotorized trails, designated ski and snowmobile routes) on wildlife using a portion of two National Forests in Washington as a case study. After identifying focal management species (for example, grizzly bear) or species groups (for example, riparian-associated species), management units of an appropriate scale were delineated for each species or species group. An extensive literature review was then conducted to determine previously documented road and trail impacts on these species. Using Geographic Information System (GIS) technology, spatial models were developed for each species to assess the relative level of human disturbance in each management unit. This information can be used to inform future decisions on road and trail construction and placement. The authors urged managers to monitor focal species' populations in areas near and far from roads and trails and to adjust the spatial impacts models accordingly, and they presented a hypothetical application of this adaptive management process.

Janis, Michael W.; Clark, Joseph D. 2002. **Responses of Florida panthers to recreational deer and hog hunting.** Journal of Wildlife Management. 66(3):839-848.

Annotation: See section III.A.3. Page 28.

Kasworm, W. F.; Manley, T. F. 1990. **Road and trail influences on grizzly bears and black bears in northwest Montana.** International Conference on Bear Research and Management. 8:79-84.

Annotation: In and around Montana's Cabinet Mountains Wilderness, radiolocations from 26 black bears (*Ursus americanus*) and three grizzly bears (*U. arctos*) were analyzed to determine the seasonal effects of roads and trails on bear habitat use. In the spring and early summer, black bears avoided habitat within 274 m of open roads and 122 m of trails. In the late summer and fall, black bears avoided habitat within 914 m of roads and 305 m of trails. In both seasons, grizzlies avoided habitat within 914 m of open roads and 122 m of trails. Sexual differences in road and trail avoidance were noted for black bears but not for grizzlies. Avoidance of high-quality habitat near roads and trails may limit the opportunity for individuals to obtain food and lead to greater intraspecific competition as bears are displaced into more remote areas.

Lacki, Michael J. 2000. **Effect of trail users at a maternity roost of Rafinesque's big-eared bats.** Journal of Cave and Karst Studies. 62(3):163-168.

Annotation: See section III.C.2. Page 33.

Mace, Richard D.; Waller, John S. 1996. **Grizzly bear distribution and human conflicts in Jewel Basin Hiking Area, Swan Mountains, Montana.** Wildlife Society Bulletin. 24(3):461-467.

Annotation: See section III.A.1. Page 26.

Merrill, Evelyn H. 1978. **Bear depredations at backcountry campgrounds in Glacier National Park.** Wildlife Society Bulletin. 6(3):123-126.

Annotation: Ecological and human-use variables at 56 backcountry campgrounds were tested for correlation with the number of bear incidents occurring in each campground. Fifty total incidents involving black bears (*Ursus americanus*) and grizzly bears (*U. arctos*) occurred over the 8-year study period. Campgrounds located in mature forest, within 5 km of a developed area, and near a good fishing spot had higher incident rates. In addition, campgrounds that had large party limits, allowed open fires, and were in a deteriorated condition (an indication of past use intensity) had higher incident rates. Bears were attracted to intensively used areas where food scraps were available (for example, refuse in open fire pits and fishing entrails). Several management recommendations were made such as locating campgrounds away from lake shores to discourage the disposal of fish entrails in the campground, requiring the use of self-contained stoves, and providing education to backcountry users on proper camping practices.

Miller, James R.; Hobbs, N. Thompson. 2000. **Recreational trails, human activity, and nest predation in lowland riparian areas.** Landscape and Urban Planning. 50(4):227-236.

Annotation: See section III.F. Page 42.

Miller, Scott G.; Knight, Richard L.; Miller, Clinton K. 1998. **Influence of recreational trails on breeding bird communities.** Ecological Applications. 8(1):162-169.

Annotation: See section III. F. Page 42.

Montopoli, George J.; Anderson, Donald A. 1991. **A logistic model for the cumulative effects of human intervention on bald eagle habitat.** Journal of Wildlife Management. 55(2):290-293.

Annotation: Based on the input of eight experts on bald eagle behavior (*Haliaeetus leucocephalus*), the authors developed a model that predicted the amount of foraging and perching habitat available to bald eagles along the Snake River in Grand Teton National Park, Wyoming. The predictor variables in the model represented five categories of human use along the river (for example, number of non-motorized boats per 1,600 m). To validate the model, the amount of habitat in 5-km river segments was predicted using data on human use levels on the river. The eight experts reviewed the predictions and concluded that the model effectively represented eagle habitat along the river. Managers from the Park and the Bridger-Teton National Forest have employed the model in decisions involving quarry and road pullout construction.

Purves, Helen D.; White, Clifford A.; Paquet, Paul C. 1992. **Wolf and grizzly bear habitat use and displacement by human use in Banff, Yoho, and Kootenay National Parks: a preliminary analysis.** Banff, Alberta: Canadian Parks Service. 49 p.

Annotation: Within three National Parks in the Canadian Rockies, the authors estimated the displacement of gray wolves (*Canis lupus*) and grizzly bears (*Ursus arctos*) from suitable habitat due to human activity. For both summer and winter, areas of human activity were delineated on a map as follows: (1) point source (for example, backcountry campsite or picnic area), linear (for example, road or trail), or polygon (for example, townsite or ski area) and (2) use level based on the number of persons using point and polygon locations and the traffic volume for linear locations. The type or timing of activities was not specified. Habitat suitability models were developed for each species, and actual habitat use by radiomarked individuals verified the accuracy of the models. Both species, particularly grizzlies, avoided areas of suitable habitat when human use exceeded a certain level. The authors suggested that increased human activity be accommodated in areas where displacement has already occurred and discouraged in areas where displacement has not yet occurred. In addition, important wildlife travel corridors should be protected.

Ream, Catherine H. 1979. Human-wildlife conflicts in backcountry: possible solutions. In: Ittner, Ruth; Potter, Dale R.; Agee, James K.; Anschell, Susie, eds. Recreational impact on wildlands—proceedings of a conference; 1978 October 27–29; Seattle, WA. Publ. No. R-6-001-1979. Portland, OR: U.S. Department of Agriculture, Forest Service, Pacific Northwest Region.

Annotation: See section IV.A.1. Page 50.

Thurber, J. M.; Peterson, Rolf O.; Drummer, T. D.; Thomasma, S. A. 1994. Gray wolf response to refuge boundaries and roads in Alaska. Wildlife Society Bulletin. 22(1):61-68.

Annotation: During a 5-year period on the Kenai National Wildlife Refuge, locations of radiocollared wolves (*Canis lupus*) were analyzed to evaluate wolf response to roads within the Refuge and human activity adjacent to the Refuge. Seventy percent of the locations were recorded during the winter. Wolves appeared to avoid a 2-km band along one gravel road receiving substantial use by oilfield workers and the general public. Prey availability probably did not influence this response because moose were common in a large burned area along the road. In contrast, two lightly used gravel roads appeared to serve as wolf travel corridors. One road was closed to public access, and the other remained unplowed during the winter. Along the western boundary of the Refuge, wolf use dropped off sharply beyond the boundary. The authors hypothesized that wolves were avoiding human settlements adjacent to the Refuge because wintertime moose abundance was probably higher outside the western boundary. Along the eastern boundary, wolves used the undeveloped land outside the Refuge in equal proportion to the habitat inside the Refuge. Because human activity was at an annual low during the winter, the authors cautioned that wolf responses could change at other times of the year, such as the fall hunting season.

Trails and Wildlife Task Force, Colorado State Parks, and Hellmund Associates. 1998. Planning trails with wildlife in mind: a handbook for trail planners. Denver, CO: Colorado State Parks. 51 p.

Annotation: This handbook offers trail planning guidelines to minimize impacts on wildlife. Because wildlife responses and planning concerns are often complex and site-specific, the handbook offers rules of thumb, rather than fixed principles, aimed at helping managers anticipate potential conflicts. The authors list important issues to consider and appropriate rules of thumb for addressing each issue. For example, one issue is that riparian areas play a disproportionately large role in maintaining biodiversity, and a corresponding rule of thumb is to minimize the number of stream crossings. Next, a chronological sequence of action items is provided for planning and building a wildlife-friendly trail. A series of trail-design case studies are reviewed that illustrate the careful consideration of wildlife needs. Finally, an extensive list of information sources on trails and wildlife is provided including Internet resources, general references, and sources specific to Colorado trail projects.

Whittington, Jesse; St. Clair, Colleen C.; Mercer, George. 2005. Spatial responses of wolves to roads and trails in mountain valleys. Ecological Applications. 15(2):543-553.

Annotation: See section III.A.2. Page 27.

4. Managing Wildlife Behavior and Habitat

Aumiller, Larry D.; Matt, Colleen A. 1994. Management of McNeil River State Game Sanctuary for viewing of brown bears. International Conference on Bear Research and Management. 9(1):51-61.

Annotation: Since 1973, a small portion of the McNeil River Sanctuary was managed as a bear-viewing site where a restricted number of visitors observed brown bears (*Ursus arctos*) at close range. From 1973 to 1994, the number of bears using the site doubled, yet no human was injured and no bear was destroyed or relocated. The program's success was largely due to the habituation of bears to people. Habituation was defined as "reduction in the frequency or strength of response following repeated exposure to an inconsequential stimulus." Importantly, habituation was achieved without the bears becoming conditioned to human food. The authors described the degrees of habituation observed among different bears and the processes by which habituation occurred. Bear and visitor management techniques used at the Sanctuary were thoroughly reviewed and recommendations were given for establishing bear-viewing programs elsewhere.

Burger, Joanna. 1995. Beach recreation and nesting birds. In: Knight, Richard L.; Gutzwiller, Kevin J., eds. Wildlife and recreationists: coexistence through management and research. Washington, DC: Island Press: 281-295.

Annotation: See section III.E.2. Page 39.

Clark, Jay E.; van Manen, Frank T.; Pelton, Michael R. 2002. Correlates of success for on-site releases of nuisance black bears in Great Smoky Mountains National Park. Wildlife Society Bulletin. 30(1):104-111.

Annotation: During an on-site release, black bears (*Ursus americanus*) frequenting developed areas are captured and immobilized, biological data is collected, and the bears are released at the capture site. Theoretically, on-site release provides an aversive stimulus that causes a bear to avoid the area of capture. After 1 year, 85 on-site releases were considered successes or failures based on whether the bear was resighted in the area, additional management actions were taken, or relocation was required. The success rate was 58 to 73 percent depending on the criterion used to indicate success. Eleven factors were tested for their ability to predict release success. Bears that engaged in daytime nuisance behavior before capture were more likely to cause additional problems than those active at dusk or night. The authors surmised that nuisance daytime activity indicated a more habituated or food-conditioned bear. Females with young were also more likely to require further management, perhaps due to their greater nutritional demands than that of solitary males or females. The authors recommended regular, night-time monitoring of campgrounds to detect the onset of problem behavior and the need to capture nuisance bears, particularly females with young, while they are still active at night.

Ingram, Dianne K. 1994. Sequoia and Kings Canyon National Parks—black bear management techniques and program update. Proceedings of the Western Black Bear Workshop. 5:99-104.

Annotation: Similar to nearby Yosemite National Park (see Thompson and McCurdy 1994), the black bear (*Ursus americanus*) management program in Sequoia and Kings Canyon National Parks (SEKI) emphasizes proactive techniques such as bear-proof garbage and food storage facilities, public education, law enforcement, and detailed incident reporting system. Unlike Yosemite, managers continue to install bear-proof food boxes in backcountry areas receiving high visitor use and/or experiencing bear problems. Information about bears and proper camping practices is distributed to visitors using several methods: personal contact by rangers, brochures, roadside signs, bulletin boards, interpretive programs, and films. A computerized reporting system allows for better record keeping of bear incidents and observations. When bears learn to obtain human food, reactive management becomes necessary. Bear incidents are either tolerated or the bear is destroyed, based on the incident's severity as determined by a bear management committee. In contrast to Yosemite, translocation is not used at SEKI because relocated bears repeatedly return to the capture site or are killed outside of the park. Aversive conditioning techniques are seldom used because time-consuming efforts directed toward a single bear are thought to be less efficient than implementing preventative measures that protect many bears.

McGarigal, Kevin; Anthony, Robert G.; Isaacs, Frank B. 1991. Interactions of humans and bald eagles on the Columbia River estuary. Wildlife Monographs. 115:1-47.

Annotation: See section III.D.1. Page 35.

Nisbet, Ian C. T. 2000. Disturbance, habituation, and management of waterbird colonies. Waterbirds. 23(2):312-332.

Annotation: See section III.E.1. Page 38.

Romero, Michael L.; Wikelski, Martin. 2002. Exposure to tourism reduces stress-induced corticosterone levels in Galapagos marine iguanas. Biological Conservation. 108(3):371-374.

Annotation: See section III.G. Page 44.

Thompson, Steven C.; McCurdy, Kathryn E. 1994. Black bear management in Yosemite National Park: more a people management problem. Proceedings of the Western Black Bear Workshop. 5:105-115.

Annotation: Similar to nearby Sequoia and Kings Canyon National Parks (SEKI; see Ingram 1994), Yosemite's black bear (*Ursus americanus*) management program stresses proactive techniques such as public information and education, proper garbage and food storage, and enforcement of regulations. Although cables, poles, and boxes have been installed in some heavily used backcountry areas, Park managers have not expanded their use because these items impact wilderness aesthetics and require maintenance in remote areas. Instead, managers encourage backcountry campers to use bear-resistant food canisters. When bears damage property, obtain food, or act aggressively, reactive management becomes necessary. Unlike SEKI, Yosemite primarily relies on relocating problem bears, although approximately 80 percent of relocations fail when the bears are recaptured in developed areas. Given the high number of human-bear conflicts in the Park, relocation is considered preferable to killing large numbers of bears.

Witmer, Gary W.; Whittaker, Donald G. 2001. Dealing with nuisance and depredating black bears. Proceedings of the Western Black Bear Workshop. 7:73-81.

Annotation: The authors discuss a range of options for managing black bears (*Ursus americanus*) that come into conflict with people. Some traditional methods, such as increasing the hunting harvest, may no longer be socially or politically acceptable. Relocation of problem bears has become a less acceptable alternative due to its high cost, the frequent return of relocated bears to the capture site, and the typically high mortality rates of relocated bears. Repellents such as capsaicin spray (pepper spray) can be used for personal protection, but bear responses to the spray are variable. Aversive conditioning tools such as rubber bullets, chemical agents, and dogs are sometimes effective, but their use may be unacceptable to some members of the public. The authors conclude that public education, tolerance of wildlife damage, and refinement of non-lethal control methods are becoming increasingly important for bear management. Critical information needs and management challenges are also identified.

V. ADDITIONAL RESOURCES

A. WEB SITES

Aldo Leopold Wilderness Research Institute, [Online]. Available: http://leopold.wilderness.net [April 18, 2008].

Annotation: This site is the home page for the Leopold Institute, a Federal interagency research group dedicated to developing and communicating knowledge needed to better understand and manage wilderness and backcountry areas. The Institute's Strategic Plan, research project descriptions, and Institute publications (including many on recreation management) are available.

Humboldt State University Library's Page on Recreation Reference Resources, [Online]. http://library humboldt. edu/~rls/nrplanrec htm [April 18, 2008].

Annotation: This site contains an extensive list of recreation resources that are available online or through the Humboldt State University Library. Available resources and links include journals, conference proceedings, bibliographies, handbooks, manuals, databases, and wilderness-related Web sites.

Leave No Trace Principles, [Online]. http://www.lnt.org/ programs/principles.php [April 18, 2008].

Annotation: The Leave No Trace Center for Outdoor Ethics is an "educational, nonprofit organization dedicated to the responsible enjoyment and active stewardship of the outdoors by all people, worldwide." This web page describes the seven "leave no trace principles," including the sixth principle, to respect wildlife. The site also links to a variety of Leave No Trace training resources.

Montana Chapter of The Wildlife Society's Online Bibliography: Effects of Recreation on Rocky Mountain Wildlife, [Online]. Available: http://www montanatws.org/ chapters/mt/pages/page4a.html [April 18, 2008].

Annotation: This organization of professional wildlife biologists provides a partially annotated bibliography with over 1,300 references on recreation effects on wildlife. Although the bibliography is focused on wildlife species found in Montana, references on a wide range of wildlife species and geographic locations are included. Online

visitors can order hard copies of the bibliography, download an electronic copy, or search the bibliography database by keyword, author, and wildlife category. The bibliography contains summary chapters for six types of wildlife (amphibians and reptiles, birds, small mammals, semi-aquatic mammals, ungulates, and carnivores); soils, vegetation, and water; and domestic dogs in wildlife habitats. Each chapter summarizes the recreation impacts reported in the literature, provides management guidelines, and identifies information needs.

Natural Resources Research Information Page: Outdoor Recreation Research, [Online]. Available: http://www4. ncsu.edu/~leung/recres html [April 18, 2008].

Annotation: This site provides general references and links to online resources for seven outdoor recreation research topics: (1) recreation planning and management, (2) recreation on public lands, (3) visitor education and communication, (4) nature tourism and ecotourism, (5) spatial perspectives, or recreation geography, (6) recreation ecology, and (7) socio-psychological perspectives. The site also contains many links to Web sites for parks and recreation areas, specific recreational activities, government agencies, professional organizations, and recreation periodicals and publishers.

The Access Fund, [Online]. Available: http://www.access-fund.org [April 18, 2008].

Annotation: The Access Fund is a nonprofit organization dedicated to keeping rock climbing areas open by promoting responsible climbing behavior. Publications available for download at this site include an annotated bibliography on rock climbing studies (see Section V.B. *Annotated Bibliographies and Literature Reviews*), a manual for managing climbing to protect raptor nest sites (see Section IV.B.2. *Visitor Use Restrictions and Zoning*), a guide to creating a climbing management plan, and a list of existing or forthcoming agency climbing management plans or general or backcountry management plans containing guidance for climbing management. The site also provides an updated list of locations where seasonal or permanent climbing restrictions have been implemented in sensitive areas.

Recreation, Wilderness, Urban Forest, and Demographic Trends Research Group, [Online]. Available: http://www.srs fs.usda.gov/trends/index html [April 18, 2008].

Annotation: This Research Group is part of the USDA Forest Service's Southern Research Station. The Web site includes information on their research activities and previous publications, many related to wilderness recreation. The page also provides access to databases and reports for the National Survey on Recreation and the Environment (NSRE). The NRSE is an ongoing, periodic series of surveys begun in 1960 to assess outdoor recreation trends in the United States. Several reports pertain to the uses and values of wildlife and wilderness as expressed by the public in recent surveys.

Wildlands CPR [Online]. Available: http://www.wildlandscpr.org [April 18, 2008]

Annotation: Wildlands CPR is a non-profit conservation group dedicated to reducing the impact of off-road vehicle use on public lands by promoting restoration, road removal and prevention of new construction, and regulation limiting motorized recreation. The webpage provides access to a variety of documents and databases to support the restoration of wild lands, including an extensive database on the impacts of motorized recreation.

B. ANNOTATED BIBLIOGRAPHIES AND LITERATURE REVIEWS

Attarian, Aram; Pyke, Kath. 2000. Climbing and natural resources management: an annotated bibliography. Boulder, CO: The Access Fund and North Carolina State University. 56 p.

Annotation: This bibliography contains annotations for over 100 references related to rock climbing impacts and management, including a section on wildlife. Brief annotations are also provided for 25 agency (State and Federal) management plans that address rock climbing. A 2001 Supplement contains over 30 additional annotations.

Boyle, Stephen A.; Samson, Fred B. 1983. Nonconsumptive outdoor recreation: an annotated bibliography of human-wildlife interactions. Spec. Sci. Rep.–Wildlife 252. Washington, DC: U.S. Department of the Interior, Fish and Wildlife Service. 112 p.

Annotation: The authors annotate 536 references of motorized and nonmotorized recreation impacts on wildlife with a focus on terrestrial vertebrates of North America. Indexes list references by keyword, authors, species, and geographic regions. The authors also include a list of bibliographies on related topics.

British Columbia Ministry of Water, Land and Air Protection. 2002. Interim wildlife guidelines for commercial backcountry recreation in British Columbia. British Columbia Ministry of Water, Land and Air Protection: Victoria. Available online at http://www.env.gov.bc.ca/wld/comrec/crecintro html [April 18, 2008].

Annotation: These interim guidelines were developed to guide applicants for commercial backcountry recreation tenure, as well as the British Columbia government, in planning and managing commercial backcountry recreation with respect to wildlife. The 2002 Interim Guidelines have been replaced with the 2006 Wildlife Guidelines for Backcountry Tourism/Commercial Recreation in British Columbia (available online at http://www.env.gov.bc.ca/wld/twg/index.html [April 18, 2008]), which are organized by recreational activity and habitat type and are considered more user-friendly by commercial tourism operators. We have included the older interim guidelines here because they reference species-specific literature and offer species-specific management objectives, mitigation guidelines, and success indicators.

Cline, R.; Sexton, N.; Stewart, S.C. 2007. A human-dimensions review of human-wildlife disturbance: a literature review of impacts, frameworks, and management solutions. Open-File Report 2007-1111. : U.S. Geological Survey. 88 p.

Annotation: After summarizing literature on the human dimensions of wildlife management, this publication concludes with an annotated bibliography containing approximately 50 publications on human dimension and wildlife. The bibliography is presented alphabetically by author, followed by an index of readings by topic.

Cole, David N.; Schreiner, Edward G. S., comps. 1981. Impacts of backcountry recreation: site management and rehabilitation—an annotated bibliography. Ogden, UT: U.S. Department of Agriculture, Forest Service, Intermountain Forest and Range Experiment Station. 58 p.

Annotation: This bibliography has 348 annotated references pertaining to recreational impacts on soils and vegetation, rehabilitation of impacted sites, backcountry management, and techniques for minimizing recreational impacts. A list of unannotated citations includes off-road vehicle impacts and recreational impacts on water quality. Indexes list annotations by location, subject, and plant species.

Dahlgren, Robert B.; Korschgen, Carl E. 1992. Human disturbances of waterfowl: an annotated bibliography. U.S. Fish and Wildlife Service Resource Publ. 188. Jamestown, ND: U.S. Department of the Interior, Geological Survey, Northern Prairie Wildlife Research Center. 63 p.

Annotation: The authors provide 211 annotated references on human disturbance impacts on waterfowl. A wide range of human activities are included, although hunting, boating (motorized and nonmotorized), fishing, and researcher disturbance studies are most common. Indexes list references by subject, geographic location, species, and author. An online version at http://www npwrc.usgs.gov/resource/literatr/disturb [April 18, 2008] can be browsed by the aforementioned index categories.

Hall, Christine; Dearden, Philip. 1984. The impact of "non-consumptive" recreation on wildlife: an annotated bibliography. Monticello, IL: Vance Bibliographies. 45 p.

Annotation: This bibliography contains 82 annotated references on motorized and nonmotorized land-based recreation impacts on wildlife. An index table groups the references by wildlife category and indicates the type of impact reported (for example, mortality, behavioral modification, reproductive success).

Hunt, Carrie L. 1983. Deterrents, aversive conditioning, and other practices: an annotated bibliography to aid in bear management. Missoula, MT: University of Montana, Montana Cooperative Wildlife Research Unit. 136 p.

Annotation: This partially annotated bibliography presents 437 references on the use of repellents, deterrents, and aversive conditioning toward bears and coyotes; bear behavior; and human-bear interactions and encounters. Repellents are activated by people to immediately turn a bear away during a close approach or attack. Deterrents prevent undesirable behaviors before a conflict occurs (for example, bears approaching camps, orchards, or garbage dumps) and do not require monitoring or manual activation. Aversive conditioning prompts bears to avoid people or their property through the repeated use of repellents or deterrents.

Joslin, Gayle; Youmans, Heidi, coords. 1999. Effects of recreation on Rocky Mountain wildlife: a review for Montana. Committee on Effects of Recreation on Wildlife, Montana Chapter of The Wildlife Society. 307 p.

Annotation: See annotation for *Montana Chapter of The Wildlife Society's Online Bibliography* in Section V.B. Page 63.

Lee, M.; Field, D.; Schwarzkopf, K. 1984. People, human behavior and animals in parks and preserves: a working bibliography. Contract CA-9000-3-003, Subagreement No. 1. Corvallis, OR: Oregon State University, College of Forestry, National Park Service Cooperative Studies Unit. 35 p.

Annotation: The authors list over 320 unannotated references related to interactions between recreationists and wildlife in parks and preserves. Citations are categorized as follows: National Park Service policy on wildlife management, value and benefits of wildlife, human attitudes toward wildlife, interactions between recreationists and wildlife, impacts of recreationists on wildlife, nonconsumptive use of wildlife, and visitor education.

Manci, Karen M.; Gladwin, Douglas N.; Villella, Rita; Cavendish, Mary G. 1988. Effects of aircraft noise and sonic booms on domestic animals and wildlife: a literature synthesis. National Ecology Research Center Rep. NERC-88/29. Fort Collins, CO: U.S. Department of the Interior, Fish and Wildlife Service, National Ecology Research Center. 88 p.

Annotation: The U.S. Air Force and U.S. Fish and Wildlife Service jointly conducted this literature review to aid aircraft and sonic-boom impact analysis. Following a brief overview of the physics of sound and aircraft noise, sources of aircraft noise, and sonic-boom characteristics, this report summarizes literature on animal hearing and the effects of aircraft noise and sonic booms on domestic animals and wildlife. The review is organized taxonomically and includes mammals, birds, fish, amphibians, reptiles, and invertebrates.

Menning, Nancy Lee. 1994. Selected annotated bibliography of publications relevant to wildlife viewing. Tech. Completion Rep. 94-2. Missoula, MT: University of Montana, Institute for Tourism and Recreation Research. 41 p. *(Note: This document can be ordered by email at itrr@ forestry.umt.edu or by calling 406-243-5686.)*

Annotation: This bibliography contains citations related to wildlife viewing and the development of wildlife viewing programs. The authors annotate 110 of 397 citations. An index table indicates the topics covered by each reference (for example, participation levels, attitudes toward animals, recreation impacts).

National Park Service. 2005. Annotated habituation bibliography. Available: http://www.nature.nps.gov/biology/ wildlifemanagement/annotated_habituation_bibliography. pdf [2008, April 28].

Annotation: Prepared for an habituation symposium (http://www.nature nps.gov/biology/wildlifemanagement/ habituation_symposium.pdf) at the 2005 Wildlife Society's annual conference (25-29 September 2005; Madison, WI), this bibliography includes approximately 160 references that are either directly or indirectly related to wildlife habituation and management. Most of the references in this alphabetized list are annotated.

Olliff, Tom; Legg, Kristin; Kaeding, Beth, eds. 1999. Effects of winter recreation on wildlife of the Greater Yellowstone Area: a literature review and assessment. Report to the Greater Yellowstone Coordinating Committee. Yellowstone National Park, WY: U.S. Department of the Interior, National Park Service. 315 p.

Annotation: This volume summarizes the research findings for motorized and nonmotorized winter recreation effects on wildlife species found in the Greater Yellowstone Area. Individual chapters review impacts on 10 mammal species or taxa (for example, bison (*Bison bison*), mid-sized carnivores), bald eagles (*Haliaeetus leucocephalus*), trumpeter swans (*Cygnus buccinator*), vegetation, and other topics (for example, impacts of two-stroke engines on water resources). A partially annotated bibliography containing 586 citations is also provided.

Ream, Catherine H. 1980. Impact of backcountry recreationists on wildlife: an annotated bibliography. Gen. Tech. Rep. INT-84. Ogden, UT: U.S. Department of Agriculture, Forest Service, Intermountain Forest and Range Experiment Station. 62 p.

Annotation: The author provides 232 annotated references related to backcountry recreation impacts on wildlife. Citations are grouped into two categories (human impacts and harassment reduction), and the literature is briefly summarized for each category. Author and keyword indexes are also provided.

York, D. 1994. Recreational-boating disturbances of natural communities and wildlife: an annotated bibliography. National Biological Survey Report 22. National Biological Survey, Washington, DC. 30 p.

Annotation: This bibliography contains 111 annotations related to motorized and nonmotorized boating effects on wildlife, primarily waterfowl, raptors, and other waterbirds. Author and subject indexes are also provided.

CITATION INDEX

The following list of citations is intended to help readers find references to specific articles, books, book chapters, or reports that are included in this bibliography. The citations in this index are listed alphabetically, by the name of the first author. For articles that are cited on multiple pages in this document, an * marks the page containing the complete annotation.

INDEX OF RECREATION TYPES

The following index is intended to help readers locate references by recreation type. Although this reading list focuses on backcountry recreation, we have included references to the following types of motorized transport: aircraft, off-road vehicles, and snowmobiling. References on aircraft overflights have been included because these are common in some wilderness areas and National Parks. Several snowmobile papers are included because they demonstrate the use of an innovative technique for assessing wildlife responses to disturbance. Other references to motorized transport occur in readings that address both motorized and non-motorized recreation. Additionally, several papers addressing the effects of roads have been included where they either refer to roads adjacent to reserves or to roads that cut through backcountry areas of National Parks or similar reserves. Disturbance locations such as trails, rivers, lakes, and campsites are also included.

A

aircraft, 2, 17, 18, 26, 30, 31, 34, 38, 39, 65
angling, 34. *See also* fishing

B

backpacking, 11, 13, 14, 44, 55
boating, 13, 14, 17, 23, 34, 35, 38– 41 *passim*, 50, 59, 64, 66

C

camping, 1, 9, 11, 13, 14, 22, 23, 26, 35, 44, 45, 54, 55, 58, 59, 61
campsites, 14, 15, 21, 23, 49, 50, 52–54 *passim*, 59. *See also* camping

D

dogs, hiking with, 10, 28–30 *passim*, 32, 35, 40, 42, 61, 63

E

ecotourism, 13, 14, 22, 31, 37–39 *passim*, 43, 44, 63

F

fishing, 4, 9, 11, 14, 21, 22, 25, 35, 37, 40, 43, 45, 59, 64. *See also* angling

H

hiking, 1, 10, 11, 13–18 *passim*, 21–23 *passim*, 26, 28–36 *passim*, 42–44 *passim*, 50, 54, 55, 57

horses, recreational use, 1, 14, 26, 31, 32, 40, 44, 54, 55
hunting, 1, 8, 9, 14, 16, 18, 21, 22, 26–28 *passim*, 30, 33, 34, 36, 37, 39, 40, 50, 59, 60, 61, 64

K

kayaking, 1

L

lakes, 10, 11, 26, 39–41 *passim*, 43, 44, 50

M

mountain climbing, 11, 22

O

off-road vehicles, 23, 28, 43, 45, 64
off-trail recreation, 16, 29, 32, 54

P

paragliding, 15
photography, 10, 13, 14

R

rivers, 23, 25, 34, 35, 38, 59
roads, 1, 2, 7, 8, 15, 23, 26–30 *passim*, 43, 44, 53, 58, 59, 60
rock climbing, 1, 13, 14, 22, 23, 41, 44, 45, 53, 57, 63, 64

S

skiing, 1, 11, 14, 28, 29, 31
snowmobiling, 2, 17, 27, 29, 58
snowshoeing, 29
spelunking, 13, 14, 32

T

trails, 1, 10, 14–16 *passim*, 22, 23, 25–32 *passim*, 36, 37, 42, 43, 49, 52, 53, 56, 58–60 *passim*

W

walking, 29, 34, 37–40 *passim*, 42–45 *passim*
wildlife viewing, 1, 9–11 *passim*, 13, 17, 23, 27, 38, 48, 50, 51, 60, 61, 65
winter recreation, 14, 19, 20, 25, 26, 29, 31–33 *passim*, 35, 36, 39–41 *passim*, 59, 60, 65. *See also* skiing, snowmobiling, snowshoeing

Publishing Services Staff

Managing Editor · Lane Eskew

Page Composition & Printing · Nancy Chadwick

Editorial Assistant · Loa Collins

Contract Editor · Kristi Coughlon

Page Composition & Printing · Connie Lemos

Distribution · Richard Schneider

Online Publications & Graphics · Suzy Stephens

Rocky Mountain Research Station
Natural Resources Research Center
2150 Centre Avenue, Building A
Fort Collins, Colorado 80526

The Rocky Mountain Research Station develops scientific information and technology to improve management, protection, and use of the forests and rangelands. Research is designed to meet the needs of the National Forest managers, Federal and State agencies, public and private organizations, academic institutions, industry, and individuals. Studies accelerate solutions to problems involving ecosystems, range, forests, water, recreation, fire, resource inventory, land reclamation, community sustainability, forest engineering technology, multiple use economics, wildlife and fish habitat, and forest insects and diseases. Studies are conducted cooperatively, and applications may be found worldwide.

Station Headquarters
Natural Resources Research Center
2150 Centre Avenue, Building A, Fort Collins, CO 80526
(970) 295-5923

Research Locations

Flagstaff, Arizona	Reno, Nevada
Fort Collins, Colorado	Albuquerque, New Mexico
Boise, Idaho	Rapid City, South Dakota
Moscow, Idaho	Logan, Utah
Bozeman, Montana	Ogden, Utah
Missoula, Montana	Provo, Utah

www.ingramcontent.com/pod-product-compliance
Lightning Source LLC
Chambersburg PA
CBHW082147290526
45794CB00008B/3193